ESPECIALLY FOR

....

FROM

....

DATE

....

3-MINUTE
DEVOTIONS
FOR GUYS

180 Encouraging Readings for Teens

3-MINUTE
DEVOTIONS
FOR GUYS

180 Encouraging Readings for Teens

BARBOUR BOOKS
An Imprint of Barbour Publishing, Inc.

© 2015 by Barbour Publishing, Inc.

Written by April Frazier and Glenn Hascall.

Print ISBN 978-1-63058-857-1

eBook Editions:
Adobe Digital Edition (.epub) 978-1-63409-266-1
Kindle and MobiPocket Edition (.prc) 978-1-63409-267-8

Published by Barbour Books, an imprint of Barbour Publishing, Inc., P.O. Box 719, Uhrichsville, Ohio 44683, www.barbourbooks.com

Our mission is to publish and distribute inspirational products offering exceptional value and biblical encouragement to the masses.

Member of the
Evangelical Christian
Publishers Association

Printed in the United States of America.

INTRODUCTION

~~~~~~

Here is a collection of thoughts from the true Source of all inspiration and encouragement—God's Word. Within these pages you'll be guided through just-right-size readings that you can experience in as few as three minutes:

Minute 1: Reflect on God's Word
Minute 2: Read real-life application and
          encouragement
Minute 3: Pray

These devotions aren't meant to be a replacement for digging deep into the scriptures or for personal, in-depth quiet time. Instead, consider them a perfect jump start to help you form a habit of spending time with God every day. Or add them to the time you're already spending with Him. Share these moments with friends, family, and others you come in contact with every day. They're looking for inspiration and encouragement, too.

> *Your word is a lamp to guide my
> feet and a light for my path.*
> PSALM 119:105 NLT

BE THAT HERO

The integrity of the upright guides them,
but the unfaithful are destroyed.
PROVERBS 11:3 NIV

Every day there are boys looking to see what you do and how you do it. They can't explain why, but you are their role model. They didn't even ask your permission. They would probably be scared to talk to you, but you're their hero. Believe it.

You probably did the same thing. You watched someone older because you wanted to learn what it is like to be a teenager. Some things you learned were good. Other things? Not so much.

Integrity is making sure there isn't a difference between what you say and what you do. Those who want to follow in your larger footsteps will understand that a person with integrity does the right thing because it's right. There's a sense of honor that follows this standard.

It's always better to maintain your integrity than try to earn it back once it's lost.

We all grow up with heroes. Make sure your hero—the one younger boys see in you—is Jesus who is transforming everything about you. Expect a greater impact on others than you ever imagined.

Dear God, I'm not sure I want other people to pay attention to what I do. That's a lot of pressure. Because I choose to follow You I want my actions to represent You. Teach me what I need to know to become someone worth following because I have chosen to follow You. Amen.

"Count yourselves blessed every time people put you down or throw you out or speak lies about you to discredit me. What it means is that the truth is too close for comfort and they are uncomfortable."
MATTHEW 5:11 MSG

God is incredibly awesome, but not everyone believes it. When you talk about God, some people will make fun of you. When you pray to God, there is a risk of lies being spread about you. This struggle has been a part of our experience since the beginning.

Jesus makes some people uncomfortable. Many can't believe smart people follow Jesus.

These people may irritate you, and even insult you, but God says you're in good company. Pray for patience, pray for the person who irritates you, and pray for wisdom to know how to respond.

Dear God, I don't like to be irritated. It's not exactly the highlight of my week when someone makes fun of me. But You tell me to be glad when others reject me because of You. When this happens, I'm to remember they may not like my message, but they're ultimately rejecting You. Give me the strength to stand up for You and disregard the irritation. Amen.

GRUDGES AND OTHER UNHEALTHY OUTBURSTS

*Get rid of all bitterness, rage, anger, harsh words,
and slander, as well as all types of evil behavior. Instead,
be kind to each other, tenderhearted, forgiving one
another, just as God through Christ has forgiven you.*
EPHESIANS 4:31–32 NLT

It's hard to forgive people who've hurt us. While they may need
forgiveness, things like bitterness, rage, anger, harsh words,
slander, and evil behavior beg for us to indulge the desire to hurt
them in return.

Holding a grudge is like holding dynamite. At some point
someone will be hurt in the emotional explosion. Often the one
hurt (for a second time) is the grudge holder.

We want justice for the actions of others, but grace for our
own choices. We're tough on others and easy on ourselves. We
think other people should make things right, but we feel like we
don't have to because God has forgiven us.

*Dear God, grudges and other unhealthy outbursts are easy
to feed, grow well on their own, and always produce a good
crop. Bitterness grows when I'm certain I was mistreated.
Harsh words come easy. However, being kind and forgiving
means I give something to the offender that they never offered.
You came to give freedom through forgiveness and love.
Help me give to others what I receive from You. Amen.*

DILIGENCE MATTERS

*Our great desire is that you will keep on loving
others as long as life lasts, in order to make certain
that what you hope for will come true.*
HEBREWS 6:11 NLT

Bring diligence to any job and be prepared to amaze. This attitude is a unique blend of a great work ethic and a willingness to stick with the job until it's done.

Employers look for employees that can show diligence in the workplace. They can usually find a long list of candidates that want a paycheck, but finding a diligent employee is much more difficult.

Being diligent in your faith is a lot like landing a great job. Work hard, honor God, care for others, and trust that your heavenly Father will be pleased with the outcome. Perfection may not be possible, but sticking with the role of a follower of Christ is just what God wants from you.

*Dear God, give me the work ethic of the diligent. I want
to be known for doing my best, doing it honorably, and
making sure the work gets done. It's easier not to care, but
because diligence matters to You help me stick with the work
I do for others, and to the journey of following You. Amen.*

ALL IN

*If anyone, then, know the good they ought to
do and doesn't do it, it is sin for them.*
JAMES 4:17 NIV

It has been said that compromise is the art of making sure
nobody gets what he wants.

Look at it this way: God wants you to be honest. You
may want a close relationship with Jesus, but you compromise
by telling what you consider a *white lie*. You rationalize the
decision by telling yourself that everyone tells white lies, but
your compromise means that God didn't get what He wanted
(obedience) and you didn't get what you wanted (closeness with
God).

You can apply the same idea to issues like purity, honor,
thoughts, and habits. Every area of your life is filled with choices.
Every small compromise moves you away from where you want
to be.

When others tell you that compromise is normal, they're
deceiving themselves and making it much harder for you to hold
strong to the choice to love God with your heart, soul, mind, and
strength.

Doing the right thing leaves no room for compromise.

*Dear God, You want me to make room for the interests of others,
but when it comes to Your commands You never want me to make
room for compromise. I want You to have what You desire for my
life, and I don't want to get in the way by compromising what
You ask. Help me go all in when it comes to obeying You. Amen.*

JOY, PATIENCE, AND PRAYER

Rejoice in hope, be patient in tribulation,
be constant in prayer.
ROMANS 12:12 ESV

Before there were water faucets, people would go outside and use a pump to draw water from the ground. When you're thirsty, you do what needs to be done to satisfy your thirst.

Joy draws from the well of hope. Patience is produced through trial. Prayer is grown through consistency.

You'd think that joy comes from doing things that make you happy, but joy runs much deeper than happiness. Joy can be experienced on bad days, in the middle of heartbreak, and when things are at their worst. The reason this is true is that joy is energized by the hope that there will be a time when difficulties will be a thing of the past.

Patience is needed for joy to thrive because the hope that we have is all about the future. Our hope brings joy, but hope needs patience. Patience only comes by facing tough challenges.

The final connected layer is prayer. When we agree to pray regularly, we have access to the God who gave us hope, develops patience, and inspires joy. Let the rejoicing begin!

Dear God, You want me to remember that joy is something
You can enhance through the struggles I face. This doesn't
seem like good news. I like it when things are easy.
Give me the patience to hope and the hope that
inspires joy. May this prayer be a good start. Amen.

Do not be misled: "bad company corrupts good character."
1 CORINTHIANS 15:33 NIV

People often use this verse to prove you need to be very careful about who you choose to be your friends. However, the bigger picture included a church where people said that Jesus didn't come back to life after He died on the cross.

If this wrong thinking had been accepted as truth then the whole idea of following Jesus wouldn't mean much. After all, if Jesus couldn't save Himself, how could He be expected to save us?

Paul was telling the people in Corinth that those who refused to believe Jesus had the ability to save were the "bad company" that "corrupts good character."

Today the idea of bad company could easily include what we watch on TV, what we read in books, and what we listen to, and it still includes people who refuse to consider that Jesus actually paid for our sins. The things we pay attention to can either help us walk with Jesus or influence us to entertain serious doubts about truth. Learn to recognize bad company.

Dear God, help me spend more time with those who love You as well as those who want to know more about You. Help me pray for those who need to know You. Jesus lives, and because He lives, I have a Savior. I am grateful. Amen.

THE DANGER OF A BAD DAY

If we confess our sins to him, he is faithful and just to forgive us our sins and to cleanse us from all wickedness.
1 JOHN 1:9 NLT

Ever have a bad day? You might be in the middle of one right now. Nothing goes right, and everyone bothers you. You don't feel like being around people, but if you must, then no one should expect you to be polite.

The truth is, God expects you to be polite, but if you blow it He has a plan to help you set things right. First, admit you blew it. When you do He promises forgiveness.

Bad attitudes are normal. We all have them. Maybe they come when a coach makes us mad, or when family members frustrate us, or when a test score doesn't live up to our expectations.

Make things right as quickly as possible. Bad attitudes can be overcome through solid choices. Admit you were wrong, forgive others who may have contributed to the problem, and get comfortable with the fact that God is in control.

Dear God, it's no fun living through bad days.
Help me take time out and think about what You want from me.
Help me admit when I blow it, and strengthen me
to forgive others whenever needed. Amen.

I know how to live on almost nothing or with everything.
I have learned the secret of living in every situation,
whether it is with a full stomach or empty, with plenty or little.
For I can do everything through Christ, who gives me strength.
PHILIPPIANS 4:12–13 NLT

Being satisfied with what God provides is the best way to hang on when things get tough.

Paul said he lived through times when he had everything he needed, but he also lived through challenges that left him with little. He, *learned the secret of living in every situation*. That secret was satisfaction in the God who provides.

We may want to give up, throw up our hands, and admit defeat. But God didn't send us a note indicating He's no longer able to take care of things.

As long as God is in control, there's no need to panic or surrender to despair.

Because Jesus gives us strength, we can watch that strength overcome our weakness. This is where we find the encouragement to resist giving up.

Dear God, it can be easy to think everything is falling apart.
When I'm satisfied that You love me enough to take care
of me, I discover that when You're with me, there is
nothing that cannot be done if You want it to be done.
Help me trust You more and worry less. Amen.

Whatever you do, in word or deed, do everything in the name of the Lord Jesus, giving thanks to God the Father through him.
COLOSSIANS 3:17 ESV

There isn't anything you can say or do that is outside the influence of Jesus. When you show patience with a new guy in school, or when you make a choice to do something that deep down you know is off-limits—each is a choice that accepts or rejects the influence of Christ.

One of the best ways to do a quick self-check on whether you're accepting the influence of Jesus is to ask yourself if the choice you want to make would be approved by God. Some answers are not difficult. Hurting someone would result in a divine veto. Caring about others will always get a five-star review.

Doing the right thing brings satisfaction, but doing the wrong thing leads to long-term regret. Doing the right thing honors God's gift of rescue, but doing the wrong thing forgets the value of His gift.

Whatever we do will be influenced by Jesus. Will we pay attention to His wisdom?

Dear God, why does the right thing always seem like the hardest choice? It would be so much easier if You made the choice to follow You the easiest decision I'll ever make. Help me love, forgive, help, encourage, and offer hope to others. Help me do the right thing because I'm doing it for You. Amen.

IN THE NAME OF THE KING

"For I was hungry and you gave me food, I was thirsty and you gave me drink, I was a stranger and you welcomed me."
MATTHEW 25:35 ESV

Jesus was an amazing storyteller. He'd been telling His disciples about a king who spoke to two groups of servants. Some were on his left and the others on his right. To the first group, the king said that because they offered help to those in need, it was like helping Him. The second group was criticized for their lack of compassion.

Jesus made it clear He wanted His disciples to be active and involved in providing help to children, widows, strangers, and the homeless. He referred to these willing servants as righteous. However, He said that those who didn't help really didn't reflect the character of His Father.

There are many opportunities for us to help others. We work because we want to serve God, but also because by serving others we are letting God love them through our actions.

*Dear God, You made it clear You want me to help others.
It makes a difference when I understand that You love every
person I help. When I help them, I help You. When I help You,
I receive help. May I see others the same way You do
and care for them like You would. Amen.*

MOVING TOWARD WHAT JESUS WANTS

*Don't become partners with those who reject God.
How can you make a partnership out of right and wrong?
That's not partnership; that's war. Is light best friends with dark?
Does Christ go strolling with the Devil? Do trust and mistrust hold
hands? Who would think of setting up pagan idols in God's
holy Temple? But that is exactly what we are,
each of us a temple in whom God lives.*
2 CORINTHIANS 6:14–16 MSG

Christians are supposed to be different. We should think, act,
and speak differently. Our best friendships should be among
those who have made the choice to be different.

While this makes sense, it's a hard thing to follow. It's
possible to find yourself really connecting with someone who has
no intention of following Jesus. You can attempt to justify dating
people because you believe you can lead them to Christ. This
thinking puts that person above God because you've chosen
disobedience to be with them.

Unless you can walk with your date toward what Jesus wants
for your life, you will both ultimately walk different directions.

*Dear God, You want me to be set apart. When I date,
help me honor You by spending time with someone
who loves You more than me. Amen.*

PLAN, PURPOSE, AND HOPE

"For I know the plans I have for you," says the LORD.
"They are plans for good and not for disaster,
to give you a future and a hope."
JEREMIAH 29:11 NLT

Do you remember dissecting a frog, worm, or other organism in science class? Maybe that's still on your agenda of things to do before you graduate. You find various body parts that help you identify the inner workings of your specimen.

Let's dissect a verse to discover how to identify our purpose in life. In the opening we discover our purpose rests on plans God has already made for our lives. We could refuse to follow His plan, but this option always leads to regret. Next, the plans God has for us are good. God never developed a bad plan. Finally, God's plans are not only for right now, but impact the future.

The takeaway is that God's good plans should always be accepted with hope because if He knows Your purpose, has developed a plan, and promises the plan is good, then following His plan leads to the best of futures.

Dear God, Your plans give an outline to my purpose in life.
What I do is important because of who I do it for. Where I go
is important because of who is sending me. You know my
purpose. Help me follow the plans that help me see
the adventure You have for me. Amen.

HE'LL TAKE CARE OF IT

Don't worry about anything; instead, pray about everything.
Tell God what you need, and thank him for all he has done.
PHILIPPIANS 4:6 NLT

Worry is a condition of missing faith. Worry unintentionally says
you don't believe God can handle the difficulties you face. Prayer
is the intentional refusal to give worry an opportunity to convince
you to make it your superhero power.

If you're struggling with something or someone, give up on
worry. It'll never change the outcome of the time you've invested.
Thank God in advance for taking care of things.

An exceedingly wonderful peace is your gift for making a
worry deposit with God. You don't have to worry about it, and
He won't worry about it. He'll just take care of it.

How often should you worry? Never! When should you stop
worrying? Right now! How can you stop worrying? Pray! When
can you pray? Right now!

Dear God, You say I should tell You what I need, so I'm here
to say I need to stop worrying. It's easy to think about what
I've been through, what's happening right now, and the things
that could happen. I need faith enough to trust that You've
got this. Help me hold on to Your gift of peace by refusing
to hang out with worry. Amen.

REFOCUS

"When you fast, comb your hair and wash your face.
Then no one will notice that you are fasting, except your Father,
who knows what you do in private. And your Father,
who sees everything, will reward you."
MATTHEW 6:17–18 NLT

Fasting is God's idea, but it may be unfamiliar to you. Most biblical fasting is an intentional refusal to eat for a while. Fasting isn't a diet, but a discipline that gives us more time to focus on our relationship with God. We give up something in order to gain something better.

While most people think of food when they think of fasting, there are other ways to fast. You might take a break from something you really love in order to get closer to God. That could be sports, music, or even social media.

When you need to take a break, a fast may bring life back into focus.

Act normally; a fast isn't something you do to be noticed, but something you do to notice God.

Dear God, You told us that fasting is something that honors You.
Maybe a fast from the drama of the Internet can help me turn
online drama into time with You. Help me also spend
more time with trusted Christian friends and find
new opportunities to serve. Amen.

HEART NEGLECT

*What matters is not your outer appearance—the styling of
your hair, the jewelry you wear, the cut of your clothes—
but your inner disposition. Cultivate inner beauty,
the gentle, gracious kind that God delights in.*
1 PETER 3:3–4 MSG

Is modesty just a girl thing? Is lust just a guy thing? In the twenty-first century we see the need for both males and females to be modest and free of lust.

Lust should never be confused with love. Where love is giving and kind, lust takes and is demanding. Where love wants the best for others, lust is only interested in what it wants.

Modesty is seeing yourself as valuable enough not to intentionally reveal things that are not meant for others. Modesty includes the art of humility.

The Bible tells us that we can get so caught up in our looks that we neglect our heart. We can also get so caught up in looking at others that we can't think straight.

Inner beauty may take longer to notice, but for Christians it is true beauty that's been enhanced by God's character and love. This is a beauty worth finding.

*Dear God, help me understand that what I wear and how I act
affects others in positive or negative ways. Keep my eyes and
heart focused on You. Keep my mind and imagination on Your
plans for me. May You find joy in my choices. Amen.*

THE REAL YOU WILL SHOW UP

[Jesus said,] "What comes out of a person is what defiles them.
For it is from within, out of a person's heart,
that evil thoughts come."
MARK 7:20–22 NIV

There's a place inside each of us that responds to good and evil.
What it spends the most time with will ultimately expose what we
really believe.

The Bible calls this place the heart—the real you that spills
over when it's full.

The heart forms character. You could spend time with
things that are true, honorable, just, pure, lovely, commendable,
excellent, and worthy of praise (see Philippians 4:8) or hung out
with things that lead to immorality, theft, murder, greed, malice,
deceit, envy, slander, arrogance, and folly (see Mark 7:22).

The heart is as quick to nurture evil as it is good. The Bible
says we can never fully understand the ways of the heart. The
heart loves emotion. The mind accepts logic. However, they can
work together to follow God—or just pretend for a while.

Your words and actions are always servants to what the
heart really believes.

Dear God, may my heart and mind be filled with You.
May my choices demonstrate things that are pure, excellent,
and worthy of praise. May I resist the influence of things that
cause me to consider greed, arrogance, and deceit normal
responses. Let me carefully choose what I allow access
to my heart. May my responses reflect a character
developed by You. Amen.

A NEW WARDROBE

Therefore, as God's chosen people, holy and dearly loved,
clothe yourselves with compassion, kindness, humility,
gentleness and patience. Bear with each other and forgive one
another if any of you has a grievance against someone.
Forgive as the Lord forgave you. And over all these virtues
put on love, which binds them all together in perfect unity.
COLOSSIANS 3:12–14 NIV

If you love to shop, there are a few things to add to your list
of *must-haves*. The Bible says we need to keep compassion,
kindness, humility, gentleness, and patience within easy reach. If
you're fresh out of these essentials just get in touch with God and
place an order.

God asks us to forgive, love, and be patient with
others. That's hard to do when your first options are revenge,
indifference, pride, cruelty, and irritation. As Christians we're
new creations, God's handcrafted people, ready for something
new. That's why He gave us a new wardrobe. Our old clothes no
longer fit with the *new us*.

There's actually no need to shop for things like compassion
and kindness because God already gave them to you. The real
question is—will you wear them?

Dear God, You're reminding me that I was made for a purpose
that's greater than what others believe. You want me to do
more than I ever could on my own. You want my outward attitude
to reflect the new thing You're doing inside me.
Help me cooperate. Amen.

DON'T BE A BAD ACTOR

If anyone boasts, "I love God," and goes right on hating his brother or sister, thinking nothing of it, he is a liar. If he won't love the person he can see, how can he love the God he can't see? The command we have from Christ is blunt: Loving God includes loving people. You've got to love both.
1 JOHN 4:20–21 MSG

It's easy to see the value in loving God. It's also easy to believe people are too messed up to love. When we fail to love people we're refusing to follow God's second greatest command. Jesus said we should love God above all and then love everyone else (see Mark 12:30–31).

A hypocrite was an ancient actor. These were people who wore masks to disguise how they really felt. The masks represented something that wasn't true. It was meant to deceive, but being classic entertainment, the audience had them figured out—the stage was filled with hypocrites. They represented an illusion.

When we say we love God, but don't love people, we're like bad actors that can't fool anyone, and never really look like the God we say we love.

Good news—even hypocrites can change.

Dear God, help me to be authentic. That means I admit to You that it's hard to love other people. With Your help I'll do what You've asked me to do, and be who You want me to be. Amen.

WHEN STUFF BECOMES TOO IMPORTANT

Do not love this world nor the things it offers you, for when you love the world, you do not have the love of the Father in you. For the world offers only a craving for physical pleasure, a craving for everything we see, and pride in our achievements and possessions. These are not from the Father.
1 JOHN 2:15–16 NLT

What makes you special? Is it your skills in sports, your strategy in gaming, what you own, who your parents are, or where you live?

Some will do things that make them happy, view shopping as a recreational sport, examine their trophies, or catalog their stuff.

God doesn't see you as less special if you come from poverty, and He doesn't think you're better if you have lots of money.

Culture influences our perspective on worth. If we have more we think we have achieved success. The Bible tells us all the stuff, awards, and happiness we accumulate can distract us from sharing God's love when these things become too important to us. When in doubt, crave God.

Dear God, You want me to be with You forever in heaven. Culture demands I collect things that make me feel like a success, but You say I am a success when I obey You. Even when You're all I have help me remember I have enough. Amen.

A gentle answer turns away wrath,
but a harsh word stirs up anger.
PROVERBS 15:1 NIV

When you start a conversation, the words you use are just as important as how you say them. Phrases like, "What made you think. . ." or "If you hadn't. . ." or "That was stupid. . ." are like pouring gas on a fire. We all can become defensive if we feel like others assume we've done something wrong without listening to us first.

It could be that we're at fault, but criticism can convince us to lash out, return hurtful words, and express anger.

If we can begin conversations by being gentle, we may experience a different result. If we respond to others in kindness, we're likely to find the other person can't stay angry for long. It's hard to fight someone with negative words when the other person won't participate.

Some people like drama. Do something different. Refuse to start arguments and then refuse to let one continue. One decision brings peace while the other invites anger.

Dear God, You expect me to show love in how I respond to
others. Even when someone is mad at me, I have an opportunity
to respond with kindness and respect. This is a hard opportunity
to accept because it is much easier to respond in frustration.
Help me be willing to give the answers
that send anger packing. Amen.

MADE RIGHT

*Therefore, since we have been made right in God's sight
by faith, we have peace with God because of what
Jesus Christ our Lord has done for us.*
ROMANS 5:1 NLT

Olympic training standards are very high. God's standards
are even higher—He demands perfection. If you dishonor your
parents, cheat, or lie—even once—He considers any one of these
offenses the same as breaking all of His laws.

You could argue that your sin wasn't nearly as bad as
something like murder, but God looks at all sin the same way.
One sin equals total guilt.

We couldn't save ourselves, which is why it's so important
that Jesus came to earth. He was the only perfect sacrifice
acceptable to God. He willingly sacrificed Himself to pay the
penalty for our choice to sin.

After Jesus rose from the dead we were invited to become
part of God's family. God accepted the sacrifice of His Son,
Jesus, so there was no longer a reason for God to declare us
guilty (see Romans 8:1).

*Dear God, Your Son, Jesus, made us right in Your sight.
We can experience peace knowing You accept us. I want to
show gratitude by obeying You so I can become more like You.
When I fail, You will forgive, but I think if You could make the
choice for me, it would be obedience—every time. Amen.*

THE IMPORTANCE OF GOD'S WORD

*God means what he says. What he says goes. His powerful
Word is sharp as a surgeon's scalpel, cutting through everything,
whether doubt or defense, laying us open to listen and obey.
Nothing and no one is impervious to God's Word.
We can't get away from it—no matter what.*
HEBREWS 4:12–13 MSG

When a company makes a cell phone, they develop an owner's manual or guide to help new users learn the benefits and limitations of the device. The same is true for cars, dishwashers, and lawn mowers. It's uncommon for someone to argue that the company really didn't understand what they were talking about when developing the manual.

God's Word is *His* word. He inspired the writing of the Bible, and it contains truth about the Maker of everything known and unknown. The Bible should receive more respect than any other owner's manual because it contains *God's* plan, truth, and life.

Even those who don't believe the truth of God's Word can't get away from what's written. It's almost as if God gave each of us a heart that will always keep looking for the truth only God offers.

*Dear God, give me a hunger to know what You've said in Your
Word. Help me think about Your words enough that they find
a place in my heart and mind and make their way into my
conversations with others. Thanks for never
leaving me in the dark. Amen.*

BETWEEN HERE AND THERE

When I was a child, I spoke like a child, I thought like a child,
I reasoned like a child. When I became a man,
I gave up childish ways.
1 CORINTHIANS 13:11 ESV

Babies make cute faces, emit sounds that make us laugh, and are generally adorable. But when a teenager acts like a baby the cuteness factor disappears. Parents expect their little bundle of joy to eventually take a first step, say a first word, eat solid food, clean up the bedroom, and get a job.

No one is comfortable around someone who looks like he's a young man, but acts like a two-year-old. Growing up is hard, and it takes patience and practice to drive selfish pride away long enough to see the value in others.

As you grow up you'll realize it's possible to make right choices even when you don't feel like it.

You live between where you once were and where you'll eventually be. There's tension as you move toward that new place, but you can't stay where you are. Use God's Word as your road map.

Dear God, thank You for helping me see early in life
that things change. I'm not the same as I was five years ago,
and five years from now I'll be much different. You made me
to grow. Help me put away childish things so that
I can become a man after Your heart. Amen.

NATURE'S TESTIMONY

*For ever since the world was created, people have seen
the earth and sky. Through everything God made, they can
clearly see his invisible qualities—his eternal power and divine
nature. So they have no excuse for not knowing God.*
ROMANS 1:20 NLT

All of creation testifies to the nature of God. To get to know God,
we read the Bible and pray and go to church and do all the
normal stuff Christians are "supposed" to do. But have you ever
reflected on nature and what it shows you about God?

Try it! What does a sunset tell you about God? Sunsets show
me that God has an artistic nature. He loves color and variety—
he is a master artist that likes to paint the sky. Sunsets also reveal
to me the faithfulness of God. The sun rises and sets—every day,
without fail. He is steady. He is faithful. We can always count
on Him.

What do you learn about God from nature? What does
grass teach you? Trees, flowers, ants? The ocean, mountains,
prairies? Lions, cows, and dogs? As you go about your day, take
time to observe the nature around you and contemplate what
invisible qualities it reveals to you about God.

*God, it's so amazing to think You've hidden a piece
of Yourself in every part of creation. Open my eyes
to see You in the nature around me. Amen.*

BODY IMAGE

*Don't you realize that your body is the temple of the Holy Spirit,
who lives in you and was given to you by God? You do not
belong to yourself, for God bought you with a high price.
So you must honor God with your body.*
1 CORINTHIANS 6:19–20 NLT

When we think about body image, we often consider things we
believe are lacking or seem the wrong size. We obsess about
proportions, strength, and whether people like the way we look.

From God's perspective body image means something much
different. Our bodies won't last forever. We'll be in heaven one
day and God wants to prepare us now for what life will be like
there.

The Holy Spirit is another of God's great gifts. Jesus calls
Him our Helper. He warns us when we consider bad choices.

God calls our bodies the temple of the Holy Spirit, so what
we do with our bodies either keeps His house in shape or makes
it less livable.

Body image shouldn't be about how we or anyone else
views what's outside, but about how we treat every part of where
the Holy Spirit lives.

*Dear God, if every part of me is Yours, then I should treat my
body with respect because it's where Your Spirit lives until
I get to heaven. Help me care more about what You think
of my body and less about the opinion of others.
May my opinion about myself match Yours. Amen.*

"HONEST" FAILURE

God can't stomach liars; he loves the company of those who keep their word.
PROVERBS 12:22 MSG

◇◇◇◇◇◇◇◇◇◇◇◇◇◇◇◇◇◇◇◇◇◇◇◇◇◇◇◇◇◇◇◇◇◇◇◇

Keeping your word can be inconvenient. When circumstances change and it's no longer easy to fulfill our agreement, we can decide we're no longer obligated to keep our promises. This could be a promise to your mom or dad to clean your room. It could be a promise to a brother, sister, friend, or teacher. Maybe they're still waiting.

We may mean well, but our intentions don't mean much if we always seem to find a way to get out of a promise.

Keeping your word can cost more than you want to pay, but the payment will be worth it even if you don't think so immediately.

A broken promise is a nice way of saying a lie was spoken. Keeping a promise gives a greater opportunity for others to trust us. If we're reliable then closer friendships can develop, more responsibility will be offered, and we'll gain a good reputation.

Dear God, You don't want me happy just being a promise maker. Keeping my word is important for me, and it's important to You. If I am ever to be a leader help me be faithful to provide an example of what it looks like to keep promises. You always have. Help me do the same. Amen.

GRACE, MERCY, AND PEACE

*Grace, mercy, and peace, which come from God the Father
and from Jesus Christ—the Son of the Father—will continue
to be with us who live in truth and love.*
2 JOHN 1:3 NLT

Can you tell the difference between mercy and grace? See if this helps. Mercy is being forgiven when punishment was the best you could expect. Grace is being given the undeserved right of a child of God.

It looks like this. Imagine a young girl caught stealing from the royal garden. Mercy is what set her free after breaking the law. Grace is what allowed her access to everything in the kingdom—including the garden.

Christians offer mercy by forgiving others for hurtful behaviors. We offer a sense of grace by treating other believers as equal children of God. We can be gracious to those still seeking Jesus.

God offers peace along with mercy and grace. When we know we're forgiven, and when we're sure we are God's children, what is there to worry about? Peace is the result of knowing God is our Father.

Dear God, what could be better than being forgiven and then made a part of Your family? You are amazing, and Your gifts are incredible. Let me rest in Your peace knowing if You can forgive and then give me a forever home, You can take care of everything else. Amen.

FAITH VS. WORKS

So you see, faith by itself isn't enough.
Unless it produces good deeds, it is dead and useless.
JAMES 2:17 NLT

We're saved by faith—we can't earn our salvation—but good deeds are supposed to be a measuring stick for our faith? I'm confused!

It's like this: salvation is only possible through God's grace. We can't do anything on our own to be "good enough" to enter heaven. But once we *are* saved, we should naturally perform good deeds as proof of our faith and God's transforming work in our life.

Or think of it this way: you can do all the homework you want in the summer, but that homework isn't why your school accepts you in the fall. However, once school starts, teachers *do* expect you to complete your homework.

Grace and deeds work the same way. You can do all the good works you want, but they won't admit you into heaven. Only acceptance of God's grace gets you in. But once you're adopted as God's child, you're expected to do good things.

Read James 2:14–18. Are your faith and good deeds out of balance? How?

Lord Jesus, please free me from feeling like I have to do good things to earn Your approval. It's such a relief to know I already have Your approval through the sacrifice of Your Son, which covers me. Help my good deeds be a reflection of Your grace in my life. Amen.

ONLY ONCE

No discipline is enjoyable while it is happening—it's painful!
But afterward there will be a peaceful harvest of right
living for those who are trained in this way.
HEBREWS 12:11 NLT

The coach makes you run a little longer, a teacher adds an extra assignment, you're grounded, work isn't going well, and you wonder if you'll ever get it right.

Whether you're corrected or you choose to submit to self-discipline the result is significant. Whatever discipline you endure (excluding physical abuse) is conditioning and training for a better future.

Learning better ways to deal with personal choices is the reason for discipline. When you learn from mistakes you have no excuse to make them again. When you choose the same mistake it becomes a habit, and the habit influences your character.

Discipline never feels good, but will lead to growth. The sooner you learn from your mistakes the less you will need to repeat the lesson. Someday you can look back at a peaceful harvest of right living for those who are trained in this way.

Dear God, help me learn that the outcome of a bad decision will always be bad. You are training and conditioning me for the race of my life. Help me respond in a way that honors You and shows that I am committed to learning from my mistakes. Amen.

I THOUGHT I COULD TRUST YOU

*Watch your tongue and keep your mouth shut,
and you will stay out of trouble.*
PROVERBS 21:23 NLT

Some secrets you hear should be passed on to an adult. For instance, if someone tells you he is thinking of hurting himself or someone else, you should seek help.

Too often someone will ask us to keep a secret. We make a promise, but then go tell someone, reminding the next person it's confidential. That person then does the same thing, and soon everyone knows.

Secrets are meant to be private. Your friend may be trying to understand a struggle he or she is going through before deciding to trust you with the problem. However, when you let the details leak, it only convinces your friend that he or she made a mistake to trust you.

If you feel you absolutely must tell someone, make sure it's a trusted adult who can help. Passing information on to other people your own age only ruins friendships, increases frustration, and invites unwanted trouble.

With social media people can post details of every part of their life. If someone shares private details with you, it's never meant for the news feed.

*Dear God, help me be a good friend. If someone needs help
then I should get help. If someone just wants to talk through
issues then I should keep my mouth shut. I can always talk
to You about any problem. May I use my mouth to ask
for Your help in every situation. Amen.*

SPEECH THERAPY

Moses said to the LORD, "Oh, my Lord, I am not eloquent, either in the past or since you have spoken to your servant, but I am slow of speech and of tongue." Then the LORD said to him, "Who has made man's mouth? Who makes him mute, or deaf, or seeing, or blind? Is it not I, the LORD? Now therefore go, and I will be with your mouth and teach you what you shall speak."
EXODUS 4:10–12 ESV

Maybe you get nervous in front of people, or maybe you sit in the crowd and can't understand why someone would have a problem being in the spotlight.

Moses was nervous in front of people. You'd think he'd enjoy being noticed. He grew up in the palace of the Egyptian pharaoh, but as an adult Moses wanted to see his family released from slavery. God sent Moses to speak to Pharaoh. What was Moses' response? It was something like, "Dear God, I get tongue-tied. I won't be very good at this."

Does it sound like Moses was shy? Maybe. God chose Moses, but promised He could help Moses with the words he needed to say. Moses soon became something other than a shy nomad. Moses led his people out of Egypt toward the land God had promised them.

Dear God, help me speak when I'm afraid. Help me find friends in spite of my fear. You helped Moses. Would You please help me? Amen.

LOVING WITHOUT THE "IFS"

*[Jesus said], "this is my command: Love one another
the way I loved you. This is the very best way to love.
Put your life on the line for your friends."*
JOHN 15:12–13 MSG

Loving unconditionally is loving without the "ifs." The "ifs"
are the conditions we place on our gift of love. If you love
unconditionally then the other person doesn't need to do anything
but accept your gift.

Loving unconditionally isn't just something for husbands and
wives. It's true for friendships, helping others, or visiting someone.

It seems everyone has love conditions. When you actually
do love without demands, someone might say, "I owe you." Even
they understand that most people expect something in return. It
can be hard to convince them there's nothing to owe.

God loves us that way. We had nothing to offer God, but He
sent Jesus to love us enough to save us (see Romans 5:6). God's
love never says, "If you'll just get your life together. If you'd just
try a little harder. If you'd just stop being something less than
perfect." When we actually accept His love, He cares enough to
invite us to a better way of living.

*Dear God, I'm grateful You love me without any "ifs."
I accept Your love, and I ask You to help me share that love
with others. May I never place demands as a condition
for really loving anyone You created. Amen.*

Samuel did not yet know the LORD because he had never had a message from the LORD before. So the LORD called a third time, and once more Samuel got up and went to Eli. "Here I am. Did you call me?" Then Eli realized it was the LORD who was calling the boy. So he said to Samuel, "Go and lie down again, and if someone calls again, say, 'Speak, LORD, your servant is listening.'"
1 SAMUEL 3:7–9 NLT

"I don't know what God wants me to do!"

Finding God's direction for your life starts by asking—and then listening. Hearing God's voice takes practice. Even the famous prophet Samuel couldn't recognize God's voice in the beginning! But God kept speaking, and eventually Samuel learned to recognize His voice.

It's hard to listen when we pray. But don't give up! God will keep speaking until you learn to hear Him. Sometimes He'll speak to our inner spirit, sometimes His direction comes through scripture or wise counsel from others, and sometimes we'll know His will through open and closed doors or a strong sense of peace. The more you practice listening to God, the more you will hear Him. So get going, man!

Lord, help me to distinguish Your voice from other voices and know when You're speaking to me. I'm so glad You keep speaking until I finally hear You. What do You want to say to me right now? Amen.

"Let your light shine before others, that they may see your good deeds and glorify your Father in heaven."
MATTHEW 5:16 NIV

If you are a sports fan, you represent your team, show up for the games, and buy team sportswear. You know the players, coaches, and mascot. People know you're a fan. You can talk about key plays in the last game, and you wear your colors proudly.

Should you be less engaged when following Jesus? Review the playbook (Bible), learn the players (know the stories), understand the rules (accept God's commands), and cheer on the home team.

Live your life in such a way that, if the rest of the world lives in darkness, then it will know who you represent by the light your life reflects. Some may want to learn more about what changed you while others pull back into the darkness.

If you make room to hide who you are, then you may not be representing Jesus, but simply admiring Him from a distance. Jesus wants us to be "all in."

You have things to learn, people to love, joy to share, hope to pass along, and mercy to distribute. Time to break huddle and get in the game.

Dear God, You've given me a responsibility to let others see You through my words, actions, and life. Let me shine Your perfect love even in my imperfection. Help me never be ashamed of You. I'm Yours, and I'm honored to be Your child. Amen.

People who work hard sleep well, whether they eat little or much. But the rich seldom get a good night's sleep.
ECCLESIASTES 5:12 NLT

"I'm so *bored*!" you moan.

"Then find something to do," says your mom.

Sound familiar? God designed us to work. He created Adam and Eve and placed them in the Garden of Eden to tend it. He never meant for us to have a life of laziness and leisure. When you work hard, even if it's not fun, you end the day feeling satisfied and sleep well. But when you sleep all day and lounge around doing nothing—you often have a hard time going to sleep at night.

Rest and leisure aren't bad things—God even commands us to have a day of rest each week. But too much rest leads to laziness, which is definitely a bad thing (see Proverbs 10:4, 26; 12:24; 13:4; 21:25).

The next time boredom hits, examine your life. Why are you bored? Have you had too much leisure time and you're left feeling restless, lazy, and unproductive? Find some work to do, whether it's a job, helping out around the house, volunteering somewhere, or participating in a physical activity. Get moving, and you'll be a lot happier—and less bored—person!

Ugh. Lord, when I'm bored, doing some kind of work is usually the last thing I want to do. Help me learn the value of work— and to have a good attitude about it. Amen.

FORGIVENESS FOR LAWBREAKERS

If we claim that we're free of sin, we're only fooling ourselves.
A claim like that is errant nonsense. On the other hand,
if we admit our sins—make a clean breast of them—he won't
let us down; he'll be true to himself. He'll forgive
our sins and purge us of all wrongdoing.
1 JOHN 1:8–9 MSG

Some people have a problem saying the words, "I'm sorry." They may realize they've offended someone, but ignore the issue and try to avoid making the mistake again. That approach won't work with God. His forgiveness comes when we admit we've sinned.

God wants us to understand when we've made wrong choices. He wants us to agree with Him that His forgiveness is necessary. If we never say we're sorry, we're hanging out with pride and that never brings us close to God.

We need forgiveness. We can't just try to do better next time. Sin requires that we acknowledge we're lawbreakers in need of forgiveness. Because we sin we need to admit the truth and accept the love of a forgiving God.

Dear God, it's no fun to come to You and admit I've blown it—
again. Yet that's what You want. Help me to be honest about
my actions and return to You every time I run away. Amen.

HARD HEARTS AND JADED EXPECTATIONS

*Faith is the confidence that what we hope for will actually
happen; it gives us assurance about things we cannot see.*
HEBREWS 11:1 NLT

We all have doubts. Sometimes we question whether good things
will ever happen. We doubt that someone who said they'd be
there for us will really show up. We live in a continual state of
"I'll believe it when I see it." These are perfect conditions for a
hard heart with jaded expectations. You can easily believe it's
normal for other people to let you down, that there is nothing you
can really trust, and there's very little to look forward to.

Faith is deciding to believe all the good things that God
promised before they actually happen. It's easier to make this
decision because God has already kept so many promises. He
has proven He's more than trustworthy, His Son gave His life to
reclaim you from a past recognized for your sin choices, and He
has a future that is beyond awesome.

With God, faith means you can be certain that He will do
what He said He would do.

*Dear God, I can't respond well to You when my heart is hard.
Help me find the places in Your Word where I can discover
proof of the promises You've kept. Help me remember
Your answers to prayer—time after time. Amen.*

RESPONSIBILITY IN ACTION

Don't be naive. There are difficult times ahead. As the end approaches, people are going to be self-absorbed, money-hungry, self-promoting, stuck-up, profane, contemptuous of parents, crude, coarse, dog-eat-dog, unbending, slanderers, impulsively wild, savage, cynical, treacherous, ruthless, bloated windbags, addicted to lust, and allergic to God. They'll make a show of religion, but behind the scenes they're animals. Stay clear of these people.
2 TIMOTHY 3:1–5 MSG

Jesus is coming back someday. Every generation has looked forward to His return. It seems like we're always faced with the bad choices of people around us. That can be a problem if we hang out with bad influences.

Take a look at the long list of choices and attitudes common even among those who say they love God. They care about themselves, their stuff, and their desires. They don't really want what God loves. They chase whatever amuses them at the moment.

How do we deal with people like this? First, we pray for them and for ourselves. We can't make decisions for other people, but we can take responsibility for our own choices. You never have to do *anything* God has warned against. You're always free to make the right choice.

Dear God, help me accept the responsibility for my own actions. May my decisions bring honor to Your name. Amen.

EMBRACE THE EXPECTATION

God is able to bless you abundantly, so that in all things
at all times, having all that you need, you will abound
in every good work.
2 CORINTHIANS 9:8 NIV

Sons are expected to do certain things. This usually includes duties related to trash, dirty socks, and grass removal. Students are expected to understand verbs, the construction of essays, and of course the Pythagorean theorem. Marching band members read sheet music, know how to play their instrument, and put one foot in front of the other while reading music and playing an instrument. Are there fewer expectations for a Christian?

For every expectation God has for you He will always provide a motivation for you to do what He asks. When God says you should forgive others, He offers you grace. When God asks you to love others, He reminds you what Jesus did to deliver you from the penalty of sin. When He asks you to share your story, He reminds you that without Him there would be no story.

When you embrace the expectations God has for you, remember He's always willing to help you and give you what you need.

Dear God, I can always expect You to be faithful, loving, generous, merciful, and kind. Help me be a son who follows his heavenly Father by reflecting who You are, and accepting the reasons You give for me to live up to Your expectations. Amen.

DARK HATRED NEEDS LIGHT

Anyone who hates a fellow believer is still living and walking in darkness. Such a person does not know the way to go, having been blinded by the darkness.
1 JOHN 2:11 NLT

Loving people is one of God's greatest commands. Love is a choice we make to show that we follow God. When we think about loving other people, it's easy to think it just includes people who probably don't know Jesus and need to see what God's love looks like.

It's possible to hang around other Christians, see their faults, and end up hating them for their failures, mannerisms, and pride. Sometimes we don't even need to find fault to hate another Christian.

If you find yourself in this dark place, God's Word says you've turned your back on the light of Jesus. In that darkness you'll discover it's very hard to see where God wants you to go. You'll also find it hard to experience joy, peace, and satisfaction.

Christians should spend time together. Making the choice to love another Christ follower may be a key to your own spiritual health. It'll definitely improve your vision.

*Dear God, You're not a God of hatred, but love.
That love isn't just for those who need to know Your Son,
but those who already do. Help me love my Christian
family even when they get on my nerves. Amen.*

NO APPLAUSE FOR ABUSE

You do not have because you do not ask God. When you ask, you do not receive, because you ask with wrong motives, that you may spend what you get on your pleasures.
JAMES 4:2–3 NIV

All abuse is the result of people not getting what they want. They might want access to a better job, higher grades, or nicer car, and when they don't get it they take out their frustration on someone who may have had no impact on the decision.

The one being abused may never understand the reasons behind the behavior. He or she may even assume responsibility for the abuse. Never believe it.

All abusers want their own way. They don't talk to God because they know their ambitions don't line up with His plan. With God there is no applause for abuse.

Dear God, I don't want to be selfish. If wanting my own way means I am more likely to hurt other people, then I need to desire Your way more than any plan of my own. Help me always choose love over violence. Amen.

> *If you are faithful in little things, you will be faithful*
> *in large ones. But if you are dishonest in little things,*
> *you won't be honest with greater responsibilities.*
> LUKE 16:10 NLT

"I don't know why they don't trust me."

Have you ever thought that before? You believe you can handle greater responsibilities, but all you get are ones that someone much younger could do without a problem. You think you're much too old for such minor responsibilities.

God is clear. If you refuse to take care of small things, then you shouldn't expect anyone to give you big responsibility.

It can seem humiliating to feel like you should be doing more grown-up jobs, but you're treated like you're still in preschool.

The quickest way to move forward is to make sure you *always* do the jobs that you're asked to do—even when they seem below your ability. This is what faithfulness looks like. It's more than just one-time obedience. Make it a life pattern and watch the opinions of others change when it comes to your ability—and responsibility.

Dear God, You want me to be reliable, dependable,
and responsible. This is what You call faithfulness—and You
invented it. Help me do what I'm asked, when I'm asked,
without being asked twice. I'm moving closer to adulthood
every day. Please shape me into the person
I was always meant to be. Amen.

"You'll not likely go wrong here if you keep remembering that our Master said, 'You're far happier giving than getting.'"
ACTS 20:35 MSG

◇◇◇◇◇◇◇◇◇◇◇◇◇◇◇◇◇◇◇◇◇◇◇◇◇◇◇◇◇◇◇◇◇◇◇◇◇

She puts money in the offering at church, keeping a separate stash of cash available to help those she sees in need. Her friends think that's unusual, but she understands something they're still learning. She will remember the grateful face of the young mother who had been a few dollars short on her grocery bill, struggling with what essential item was less critical. She'll remember the joy of stepping in to help. She'll remember her decision to obey.

You may not make a lot of money. You might get an allowance and consider every dime something you can use to buy whatever you want. But when you intentionally give some of it away you will discover what she did—there's incredible joy in allowing God to do something impressive with His money.

God has given us everything we own. He doesn't need our money to keep things in good shape. Our giving is something that connects our heart to His. We give because He gave. Our generosity is a sign that we understand His heart.

Dear God, You want me to be generous. I wouldn't have anything if it weren't for You. Help me release my grip on Your money and share whenever You ask. Thanks for always being generous with me. Amen.

*Here's how you tell the difference between God's children
and the Devil's children: The one who won't practice
righteous ways isn't from God, nor is the one who won't
love brother or sister. A simple test.*
1 JOHN 3:9 MSG

God wants us to judge. This isn't judging as to whether God could love, save, or accept an individual. This is a type of judgment that looks a bit like the work of a detective and less like a judge. The Bible calls this *discernment*.

Discernment helps distinguish the difference between good and bad decisions, who'd provide a good influence and who wouldn't, and who follows God and who pretends.

Today's verse can be used to become better discernment detectives. It's an easy pass/fail test. If a person makes it a practice to live according to God's Word and loves other Christians, then they represent God's children. If they don't care what God has to say and they always find fault with other Christians, then it's possible they aren't God's children.

You will never be the final judge on anyone's life—that's God's job—but discernment can help you identify who might be a trustworthy influence.

*Dear God, You hate it when I'm judgmental,
but You encourage me to discern between good things
and bad. Help me determine what influences please
You and discern what to allow into my life. Amen.*

AN AUTHENTIC FAILURE

He said to me, "My grace is sufficient for you,
for my power is made perfect in weakness."
2 CORINTHIANS 12:9 ESV

John Wayne portrayed movie characters that were self-reliant, strong, and despised the idea of failure or weakness. While he was an admirable actor I'm not sure he's the perfect role model for what Christian manhood looks like.

Christian men understand they will fail. They understand that compared to God they are weak. Knowing this doesn't stop them from being brave and shouldn't prevent them from hitting the gym. However, it does mean they should be honest about their need for a Savior. Most of our spiritual muscles are puny.

God rescues the weak. He gives grace to the humble. He resists those who act like they don't need Him. The power of God is available once we admit we need it.

Being an authentic Christian guy means cooperating with God in life transformation by being honest enough to say you don't always get it right.

Dear God, it would be nice to say that I've never failed,
but I'd be lying. If I say I don't need You, I refuse the only strength
I can reliably access. Show Your strength in my weakness
and I will have another reason to honor You. Amen.

TAKING THE PLUNGE

"No one will be able to stand against you as long as you live.
For I will be with you as I was with Moses. I will not fail you
or abandon you. Be strong and courageous, for you are
the one who will lead these people to possess all the land
I swore to their ancestors I would give them."
JOSHUA 1:5–6 NLT

A water park near my home has several high dives. I always
wanted to jump from the highest one, but one look over the edge
had me scurrying back down the steps. No matter how much I
psyched myself up, I could never make the jump. Then one day
my dad took my hand and said he'd jump with me. I was still
freaked out, but jumping with Dad gave me extra courage.

After Moses died, God gave Joshua the huge task of leading
Israel to claim the Promised Land. That meant ousting a lot of
nations! Numerous times God reassured Joshua that He would
not abandon him and to be strong and courageous.

Sometimes God asks us to do scary things. But He doesn't
leave us to jump alone. He takes our hand and plunges right in
with us.

God, thank You for never abandoning me. Help me to be
courageous and do the tasks You ask of me, knowing
You're right there with me the whole time. Amen.

LOOKING FOR LOOPHOLES?

Better to be poor and honest than to be dishonest and rich.
PROVERBS 28:6 NLT

Watch enough movies and you might be tempted to believe that the only way to get ahead in life is to look for loopholes, lie on applications, and take advantage of technicalities. You'd almost think people *expect* you to cheat in order to reach your goals. Honesty seems to be a foreign concept.

God looks at cheating as a dishonest way to reach a goal. He says He would rather you remain poor and retain integrity than to get rich by cheating. Even if no one ever finds out, God knows and He'd still rather see your integrity intact than for you to rely on deception.

To cheat on a test doesn't reflect your real knowledge of a subject. To cheat on an application doesn't demonstrate your real experience and skills. To cheat during a game doesn't show your real athletic ability.

A lifestyle of cheating deprives you of ever really answering the questions related to your true capabilities. You will always be deceiving others. You'll always be deceiving yourself. Suddenly being poor and honest looks pretty good.

Dear God, You love honesty and despise cheating.
You can and do forgive cheating, but You want me to use honesty
in my decision-making, in my interaction with others,
and in my relationship with You. Help me view cheating
as a poor substitute for right living. Amen.

[God said to Job], "Who shut up the sea behind doors when it burst forth from the womb, when I made the clouds its garment and wrapped it in thick darkness, when I fixed limits for it and set its doors and bars in place, when I said, 'This far you may come and no farther; here is where your proud waves halt'?"
JOB 38:8–11 NIV

God brings order to chaos. Maybe this is why when someone finally accepts His gift of rescue they see that life with God makes sense.

He sets ocean boundaries. He gives each season three months. He tells day and night when to start. We feel safe when we know those boundaries are set. It would seem strange for the sun to start shining at night, winter to show up in summer, or the ocean to suddenly change locations.

Christians exist with boundaries, too. When we follow God's limits on our actions we can feel as if God doesn't want us to have any fun. The boundaries help us learn God's expectations so we're free to do what we were made to do.

Dear God, You created birds to fly, not swim. You made snakes to slither, not gallop. You made me to follow You, not live apart from You. I'll always be free when I thrive in the place You've made for me. Help me recognize boundaries are for my good, not to stop me from enjoying good things. Amen.

ONCE THEY WERE YOUR AGE

*You who are younger must accept the authority
of the elders. And all of you, dress yourselves in humility
as you relate to one another, for "God opposes
the proud but gives grace to the humble."*
1 PETER 5:5 NLT

Some adults are quick to say, "Kids get to a certain age and think they know everything." It's true; some do. Hopefully that doesn't describe you.

God wants people like you to learn from people who've lived a bit longer. When you do, you can hear some great stories, but you'll also learn some mistakes to avoid, virtues to pursue, and a few answers to questions you didn't know you had.

Never walk around feeling superior to people who are part of a generation you don't understand. They really were once your age, and they've lived through more than you have. What they know may be important to learn.

When you think you know everything, you can be sure there's a new and extremely hard lesson coming that you didn't even know you needed.

Demonstrate honor and humility. Be someone who's teachable. The lessons are more understandable when you have good teachers. Those teachers can become great friends.

*Dear God, You don't want me to be arrogant,
but You do want me to honor those who are older than I.
Help me appreciate their wisdom and the time they
are willing to spend teaching me. Amen.*

THE GRIEF ATMOSPHERE

"The LORD is close to the brokenhearted;
he rescues those whose spirits are crushed."
PSALM 34:18 NLT

Grief feels like someone threw a boulder at your heart. Grief makes you think crazy thoughts and insists things will get worse. Grief lies to you. It holds you hostage in a place of despair and pain.

It's natural to feel grief when someone dies, after a breakup, and when you leave good friends.

Grief creates an atmosphere of loneliness. Your melancholy mood tells others it's not time to get close, but to stay away. It may not be the message you intend, but it's how others respond.

God has a special message for those who grieve. He says, "I'm here to rescue you from this horrible place." While not His exact words, the truth is the same. God knows you'll need Him when grieving. He knows you need rescue when your heart is crushed. He never leaves you to go through it alone, although some people refuse His company.

Never believe there's no way out of the grief you feel. God can, does, and will walk with you through what may feel like the "shadow of death" (see Psalm 23).

Dear God, Your heart understands grief. You gave Your only
Son to rescue me. You watched Him die. You heard Him ask
why You'd forsaken Him. Yet in every grief there is new
potential for joy. Walk with me when I hurt the most.
Thank You for understanding. Amen.

ON THE OUTSIDE LOOKING IN

God does not show favoritism.
ROMANS 2:11 NLT

What if God suggested that the only people He could really love had to have a certain foot size, be able to yodel, and loved oregano more than any other herb? That would leave a lot of people unloved.

God doesn't show favoritism—we do.

We'll only like people with similar interests, looks, and skin color, while others are dismissed before we know their names.

Favoritism leads to cliques, clubs, and gangs. If you're one of the favored few, you can become a part of something that is considered elite—by the favored few.

Popular people are often popular only because a small number of people said they were. The rest just go along with it.

What if you just loved getting to know people? What if someone that seems different from you helped you learn something you didn't know before? What if you were surprised by a friendship that grew from someone you'd never thought of as a potential friend?

All people need to know God, but if we get into the habit of only talking to people that fit our qualifications, then we can't share what we know with the most people.

God doesn't show favoritism. Why should we?

Dear God, it's no fun being on the outside looking in. Help me be in the inside reaching out. Help me always remember You love everybody even when they don't accept it yet. Amen.

GROWING LIKE JESUS

*And Jesus grew in wisdom and stature,
and in favor with God and man.*
LUKE 2:52 NIV

We don't know anything specific about Jesus when he was a teenager, but Luke 2:52 gives us a brief summary. As Jesus grew from boyhood to manhood, we know he grew in wisdom (mentally), stature (physically), and in favor with God (spiritually) and men (socially). He lived a balanced life.

How do you measure up in these areas? Are you applying yourself at school and completing your homework? Are you eating healthy and participating in regular physical activity? Are you consistently spending time with God and growing in your relationship with Him? How about relationships with others? Do you initiate social activities with others or sit and wait to be called? Are you meeting new people or stuck in a clique?

As you examine each of these four areas, how do you need to bring better balance in your life? Are you favoring one or two areas over the others? Has one area totally fallen off your radar? Pick an area that most needs work in your life and set some goals to help you grow. Involve a parent or friend in your goals so they can help hold you accountable.

*Jesus, I know You were perfect and it's impossible to be just like
You when You were a teenager. But help me to follow
Your example and push myself to grow mentally,
physically, spiritually, and socially. Amen.*

OWN YOUR STUFF

*The Lord God asked [Adam]. "Have you eaten
from the tree whose fruit I commanded you not to eat?"
The man replied, "It was the woman you gave
me who gave me the fruit, and I ate it."*
GENESIS 3:11–12 NLT

God made the earth, planets, ocean, air, animals, man, and
woman. Adam was impressed. God told the couple to stay away
from a particular tree in the garden. They could go anywhere,
eat whatever they wanted, and name the animals. Then a
serpent tempted Eve to eat from the tree that was off-limits. Once
she sinned, she offered the fruit to Adam, and he, too, seemed
convinced that disobeying God made sense.

The couple had never sinned until that moment. It impacted
what they wore, how they felt, and how they related to God.

Instead of turning from personal sin, the couple made
excuses. Adam blamed Eve. Eve blamed the serpent.

There are circumstances in life that can prevent us from
understanding what God wants, but when we know the right
thing to do, we no longer have an excuse for *doing* the wrong
thing.

It's always time to own your stuff.

*Dear God, I'm tired of making excuses. You must get tired
of hearing them. Instead of trying to talk myself out
of punishment maybe I should accept your mercy, grace,
and love. This should be followed by obedience. Amen.*

*[Jesus said], "Don't pick on people, jump on their failures,
criticize their faults—unless, of course, you want the same
treatment. That critical spirit has a way of boomeranging.
It's easy to see a smudge on your neighbor's face and be
oblivious to the ugly sneer on your own. Do you have the nerve
to say, 'Let me wash your face for you,' when your own face is
distorted by contempt? Wipe that ugly sneer off your own face,
and you might be fit to offer a washcloth to your neighbor."*
MATTHEW 7:1–5 MSG

Discernment raises warning flags while being judgmental
assumes you know enough about a situation that you can say
something is true when you really have no idea.

We can decide that we want to be helpful by pointing
out every flaw we see in someone. While we feel we're being
helpful, we actually distance ourselves from others. God is their
judge. What they need is a friend. Pray for them, love them, and
if you discern there are issues to avoid, then avoid them.

Stand back and watch God work. He's done this before.

*Dear God, You gave us the cure for a judgmental attitude.
Really love people. Your love has a way of helping me
accept people in spite of faults. May I allow You
to work without my less-than-expert opinion. Amen.*

AN ACCEPTED REJECT

*He was despised and rejected—a man of sorrows,
acquainted with deepest grief.*
ISAIAH 53:3 NLT

Each person has something they want in life. It's simple, really. They want to be accepted. They want to be loved.

However, rejection always brings its two best friends— sorrow and grief. These traits cause us to hold back and refuse to interact with others because we're afraid that the cycle of rejection will happen all over again, so we risk loneliness in an effort to stop rejection.

We're never happy when we're rejected, and somehow we assume that any rejection is God's way of saying we don't matter.

We miss all the evidence that proves something else. God loved us enough to send His Son to rescue us from sin. He cared enough about us to make a way for us to be His friends. He saw something special in us that allowed Him to offer a hope for our future. We are not rejected by God. We are loved. We are accepted. We are His family.

Dear God, You have always accepted me. You never reject me from coming to You. You simply waited for me to come to my senses so I would be wise enough to boldly accept You. Thanks for being patient. Amen.

THE UNWANTED VOICE OF A THIEF

"The thief comes only to steal and kill and destroy;
I have come that they may have life, and have it to the full."
JOHN 10:10 NIV

Do you think you're valuable to anyone? We each have a seed of insecurity inside that grows up and bears fruit when we don't want it to. It's like a voice whispers, "Hey, you're still not good enough." This voice is the thief who wants to destroy our lives. Our enemy doesn't want what's good for us. He may tempt us with small changes in thinking, or he might attempt to convince us we aren't worth anything.

We should be willing to recognize that we're insecure in our thinking, but totally secure in God's love and grace.

God came to bring us a full life. He came prepared to bless us with all kinds of spiritual blessings. We find all the security we need in being His child. All our failures mean very little when compared to knowing Him and accepting the security of His love.

Dear God, Your words say that You created me, love me, and
have a future for me. I'm accepted by You—the God who made
it all. Help me live in the joy of Your acceptance.
Help me thrive in the hope of Your promises. Amen.

GRATITUDE: THE GIFT FOR EVERY OCCASION

*Give thanks in all circumstances; for this is the will
of God in Christ Jesus for you.*
1 THESSALONIANS 5:18 ESV

When you were little your parents often prompted you to say the right things with phrases like, "What do you say?" or "Wasn't that nice?" when someone gave you a gift or did something unexpected.

You may have hidden behind your mom or mumbled, "Thanks" without ever really understanding gratitude.

We don't always feel grateful until we realize the thoughtfulness that comes with every gift.

God wants gratitude to be a gift we give on all occasions. When someone shows hospitality, holds a door, or offers cold water on a hot day, the best gift we can offer is thankfulness.

Even when we don't feel as if everything is going the way we want, we should offer gratitude because things could always be worse.

When we show gratitude, we recognize the value in others, reject personal selfishness, and inspire growth in relationships.

There was a reason your parents asked you to say *thanks*. By understanding that gratitude is something you give to others, you can begin to see how many gratitude gifts you need to offer.

*Dear God, You rescued me, and I'm grateful. You offered
friendship. You gave peace, mercy, forgiveness, and love.
You have provided people who share with me,
and You are giving me daily opportunities
to show gratitude to those who gave. Thank You. Amen.*

DESTROYED BY JEALOUSY

We're blasted by anger and swamped by rage,
but who can survive jealousy?
PROVERBS 27:4 MSG

Anger is visible and harsh, rage is anger in action, and jealousy is more dangerous than both.

Jealousy is anger and rage mixed with greed, control issues, and a bit of selfish ambition to keep it focused on what it desires most.

Jealousy leads people to physically hurt and even kill others. Jealousy is never satisfied if someone has what it wants. Jealousy is blind, bold, and bitter. It has trouble seeing the logical end of its rage.

Jealousy hangs out with hate and plots deeds God repeatedly warns against. Each wears armor that resists kindness and love and will punish those who offer these gifts.

Jealousy is a monster that can't stand wisdom, won't heed warnings, and has a faulty memory.

"Where jealousy and selfish ambition exist, there will be disorder and every vile practice" (James 3:16 ESV).

What will jealousy always keep out of its circle of friends?— Satisfaction, peace, trust, forgiveness, and love. It can't entertain these guests without rethinking its existence.

Dear God, I'm at war within my own heart when it comes to following You. I can trust You to show me the way through feelings of jealousy, or be led by an enemy that wants to destroy me. Help me put aside jealousy so I can hear You. Amen.

Let the Spirit renew your thoughts and attitudes. Put on your new nature, created to be like God—truly righteous and holy.
EPHESIANS 4:23–24 NLT

Your past should only be a potent reminder of who you were and not a statement about what you are. If all of us were only judged by our past then it would be easy to believe nothing good can ever happen to us.

Jesus came to exchange what we've been for what we'll become. He came to redefine our entry in life's dictionary. Jesus knows what we can become is so much more than what we once were.

The problem is we grab on to our past and hold on tight. Maybe we think we'll miss out on something if we don't give our past a death grip. Our past is familiar. Like a favorite-but-useless shirt, we need to release our grip on a ragged past and embrace God's plan for today, tomorrow, and the day after forever.

Dear God, help me remember that my past wasn't perfect. Help me believe that my present choices are critical to the future You've planned for me. Remind me that when I follow You I will never miss out on anything that is really important. Amen.

THE LANGUAGE OF GOD'S HEART

Now is the time to get rid of anger, rage, malicious behavior, slander, and dirty language.
COLOSSIANS 3:8 NLT

Our words make an impact. You remember the old saying about sticks and stones? They can hurt a person, but words never do. This may be easy to say, but much harder to believe. Because we've all faced insecurity; the words others say about us impact our emotions and heart in a way a slap on the face can't.

Some believe what we say and how we say it is less important than allowing others to see Jesus in our lives. When we let a string of profanity flow from our lips that's strong enough to melt the screen on our cell phone, we leave people with a belief that what we say and do doesn't match who we say we are.

Because we represent Jesus, our words should sound different from what's expected. In place of criticism we speak the language of encouragement. Instead of profanity we speak blessing. Instead of gossip we speak love.

If we do that, we'll speak words others will want to hear.

Dear God, when my words are formed in anger, rage, malicious behavior, and slander, they will be so emotionally driven that they won't form thoughts that represent You. My words can clear up or confuse the best message I'll ever share. Amen.

DO NO HARM

*I plead with you to give your bodies to God because of all he
has done for you. Let them be a living and holy sacrifice—the
kind he will find acceptable. This is truly the way to worship him.*
ROMANS 12:1 NLT

God gives you an amazing number of choices. You can follow
His commands or choose to reject them. When you choose to
reject them, that choice can show up in embarrassing ways.

Your mouth can bless or curse. Your hands can promote
peace or war. Your feet can follow God or run away. Your body
can be an acceptable gift for God to use as He wants or a
personal experiment that could harm your body and testimony.
This applies to what we drink, eat, touch, smell, and look at. It
also applies to what we put into our body without concern for
what it does to our thinking or actions.

The Bible says we worship God when we dedicate our body
to the things He wants for us. His commands are for our safety
and benefit, but they are also because, in our obedience, others
may notice God for the first time.

*Dear God, because You've given me a choice,
help me understand how I can please You with my body.
May I never allow anything to come between me and the honor
of Your name. Help me avoid those things that take me
down any path that doesn't include You. Amen.*

For you created my inmost being; you knit me together in my mother's womb. I praise you because I am fearfully and wonderfully made; your works are wonderful, I know that full well.
PSALM 139:13–14 NIV

◇◇

Before you were a singer, athlete, self-proclaimed geek, student, poet, artist, son, or brother you were a creation of God. He gifted you with skills, interests, and potential. He created your "inmost being"—the part of you that's usually described as heart, mind, and soul.

Maybe you've never spent enough time discovering what you were made for, which is why you compare yourself to others and think you're just not good enough.

You've forgotten who built you. God created a sense of significance within you that shouldn't inspire pride, but gratitude. God gave you a talent, voice, longing, and love, and He's the only One qualified to understand you and satisfy your soul. And even if your body is imperfect, it is your heart, mind, and soul that are connected to eternity. That's why God spent so much time making sure it could become just what He planned for you.

Dear God, no one is just like me. You made me an original. The only way for me to be truly fulfilled is to know that You made me, and You're still waiting for me to catch up to Your purpose. Help me keep seeking Your plan. Amen.

ABUSIVE MOUSE CLICKS

There are "friends" who destroy each other,
but a real friend sticks closer than a brother.
PROVERBS 18:24 NLT

Have you ever noticed how much drama there is on social media? Pictures feature negative comments. Posts are criticized. Sarcasm flows like the Mississippi River at flood stage. You log off the computer feeling like you've just witnessed a violent crime. Maybe you participated.

Many adopt a personality that's different than their own when they post online. They post hurtful things they'd never be bold enough to say in person.

Social media isn't better or worse than TV, video gaming, or smartphones. However, there are many who are more than willing to continue the spread of bad conduct online.

We've all seen the "friends" who destroy each other. Instead, be a friend that sticks closer than a brother. Decide before you go online what you'll participate in, accept, pass along, and laugh at.

Don't be afraid to step away for a while. Ask your family for help if there's an issue you don't know how to handle. Spend time with God. He's always willing to interact with you—even when the power is out.

Dear God, help me know when to shut off social media.
May it never become more important to me than You are.
I never want to be one who hurts others through the words
I use online. Help me remember anything I post is
a reflection of my relationship with You. Amen.

WITHOUT MEANING—WITHOUT VIRTUE

We are instructed to turn from godless living
and sinful pleasures. We should live in this evil world
with wisdom, righteousness, and devotion to God.
TITUS 2:12 NLT

Flirting is usually viewed as a way to let someone of the opposite sex know you like them. The root word of *flirting* can be defined as "without meaning." Perhaps the reason for this is flirting rarely leads to long-term healthy relationships.

Girls who flirt are often thought of as without virtue. When guys flirt they are often indicating they have no real interest in a lasting relationship. They just want to spend time with girls.

The Bible calls this cycle godless living and sinful pleasure. God wants us to turn away from this path. Selfishness is at the core of flirting. The one who flirts is seeking his or her own interests and often cares little about the one with whom he or she is flirting.

Philippians 2:3 says, "Don't be selfish; don't try to impress others" (NLT). Does this sound anything like flirting to you?

Flirting can also lead you to entertain thoughts you might not usually think and cause you to lust. Flirting can indicate you have an interest in a physical relationship that's always to be saved for marriage.

Dear God, flirting doesn't show others that I want to honor You.
It doesn't show that I really love others the way You do.
Help me honor You in every relationship. Amen.

BEING DIFFERENT

But Daniel was determined not to defile himself by eating the food and wine given to them by the king. He asked the chief of staff for permission not to eat these unacceptable foods.
DANIEL 1:8 NLT

When Babylon captured Jerusalem, Daniel found himself as a slave in a foreign country. Suddenly outside of his religious comfort zone, he made a decision. Daniel was determined not to let the culture around him define what was acceptable for him. That meant firmly holding to his beliefs and finding creative solutions to get around cultural practices. Instead of accepting his plate of assigned food, Daniel asked permission to eat only vegetables and drink water instead of consuming the unclean meat and wine (see Daniel 1:11–14).

Following Jesus will always mean living differently than the world around us. The world does not and should not define our standards and boundaries. Only Jesus should be our guide. What pressures do you feel from the crowd? What decisions do you need to make in your heart? How can you creatively stand your ground without being rude or obnoxious?

Lord, sometimes it's so hard to be different. It's much easier to go with the flow instead of making myself stand out. But I know You want me to do what's right, no matter what others think. Help me to stand my ground and follow You, no matter what. Amen.

HOMEWORK

Study this Book of Instruction continually. Meditate on it day and night so you will be sure to obey everything written in it. Only then will you prosper and succeed in all you do.
JOSHUA 1:8 NLT

Homework. . .ugh! It's such a pain, especially when you can spend your time doing more fun activities. Sure, you might enjoy doing math homework or English homework, if that's your thing. No one enjoys doing homework from *every* subject. You discipline yourself to do it anyway because if you don't do your homework, you fail your classes. And if you fail your classes. . . you have to repeat your grade. No one wants to be stuck in the same grade again instead of advancing forward!

Our spiritual life is much the same way. If you want to prosper and succeed, you have to put in the work. When you study God's Word, spend time talking with Him, and stretch yourself to obey what He wants you to do, you'll advance into a deeper, fuller relationship with Him. But if you neglect your spiritual life to spend your time doing more fun things, you'll stay stuck where you are.

Does your relationship with God feel a little lacking? Buckle down and do some spiritual homework and see where it takes you!

Lord, help me to continually study Your Word and obey You so I can keep growing and not get stuck where I am. Amen.

ON-THE-JOB TRUSTING

Work brings profit, but mere talk leads to poverty!
PROVERBS 14:23 NLT

Behind your parents' occupations is a story about how they landed their jobs. Maybe they were successful with their former employer and that allowed them to get a new job. Maybe the job they have is the only one they've ever known. Maybe the economy forced them to try something new.

Your work history will have its own story, too. It starts with knowing work is important. Not just because you earn some money, but because it can help refine you into a person with a work ethic that honors your employer, does more than required, and gives your employer every reason to trust you.

When you're hunting for a job, never take an interview for granted. The potential employer isn't there for you; you are there for him. Show up on time, dress appropriately, spend time with the application, ask questions, respect the interviewer, listen carefully, and represent Jesus—the One you really serve.

God wants us to work for our benefit, and to take His love beyond the borders of familiar surroundings. Work isn't your entire story, but it plays a part.

Dear God, help me show respect to potential employers. If I get a job help me do my best. I understand that no matter where I go I'm Your representative. May I never give an employer a reason to believe Christians are bad employees. Amen.

MANAGING EMOTIONS—EMBRACING STABILITY

Take care that you are not carried away with the error of lawless people and lose your own stability. But grow in the grace and knowledge of our Lord and Savior Jesus Christ.
2 PETER 3:17–18 ESV

Relying on emotions to determine truth is dangerous. Sometimes very likable people can convince you to believe something that's not true simply because their friendship means too much to you.

Our enemy, Satan, does the same thing. He can make things look really impressive. We can be tempted to believe a lie when our emotions convince us we're looking at truth.

One statement that's been around for years is, "How could it be wrong when it *feels* so right?" God cares less about your feelings and more about your obedience.

We're flooded with issues that appeal to our emotions. It can be easy to throw common sense away in favor of beliefs that can never be supported by God's Word.

God wants stability in our lives. When we chase after the latest issues with only emotions to guide us, we shouldn't be surprised when we find ourselves off track.

Dear God, You want me to manage my emotions so I'm not unstable in what I accept as truth. Whenever I need to know truth, help me seek Your Word in spite of how I feel. Amen.

HIS PLAN IS WORTH THE WAIT

God created man in his own image, in the image of God
he created him; male and female he created them.
GENESIS 1:27 ESV

God created the first man. When He saw it was not good for man to be without companionship, He created the first woman. These two were designed to complement each other in every way, and it was good.

At some point you'll grow up, leave home, and fall in love. If you're obedient, you will save yourself for marriage. God calls you to sexual purity for the physical union of husband and wife.

Casual sex takes something meant for your future spouse and gives it to one or many.

Inappropriate touching causes your mind to entertain sexual thoughts that should be reserved for marriage.

God's design for marriage is one man and one woman who have saved their sexuality to give to each other on their wedding night (see 1 Corinthians 6:18).

Sex is a good idea created by God. It's a gift for those who are married to enjoy. It's also something that allows children to be born into a family.

Waiting is necessary so you can enjoy God's best plan for you.

Dear God, help me accept that there are things I shouldn't
fully understand about sex until I'm married. Help me accept
that the mystery is worth the wait. Help me trust that
Your plan for me is incredible. Amen.

DON'T CARRY SPIRITUAL BAGGAGE

All your lives you've let sin tell you what to do. But thank God you've started listening to a new master, one whose commands set you free to live openly in his freedom!
ROMANS 6:17–18 MSG

Habits bring freedom or slavery, life or death, satisfaction or discontentment. Some habits start early and last a lifetime. Others can result from the devastating pressure of others.

Some people have no interest in helping you achieve God's plan. If other people know you want to follow God, they may consider it an achievement to see you stumble. Once you go back on your word to God, it can be hard to return. God forgives, but wants you to turn away from sin. It's hard to see God when you're too ashamed to look His direction.

Habits form when you refuse to admit you're wrong. This spiritual baggage gets harder to carry with each passing day.

Dear God, no matter how many times I fail, help me turn back to You immediately. It may seem like I'm not moving forward, but even slow movement in Your direction is better than playing hide-and-seek. Help me seek You immediately when I make bad choices. Amen.

REGRETS

*Remember your Creator in the days of your youth, before the
days of trouble come and the years approach when
you will say, "I find no pleasure in them."*
ECCLESIASTES 12:1 NIV

The teen years are full of promise. You can't wait to drive and
have your own car. You look ahead to your future with excitement
and imagine the adventure and independence of college. Your
future is a blank canvas, and you can be anything or do anything
you want!

What most teens *don't* realize is how your choices now can
drastically affect your future. One simple choice now can have
consequences for the rest of your life that you never imagined.
Ask a teen mom how bright her future looks. Or a high school
senior who drove drunk and killed someone in a car accident.
Many teens and college students who live the wild life while they
are young come to regret it when they're older.

But if you remember your Creator and stay committed to
Him now, you're setting yourself up for success—both now
and later! Instead of looking back with regrets and feeling like
you've wasted parts of your life, you can look back with peace
and happiness and feel abundantly blessed at all the Lord has
given you.

The choice is yours—starting now.

*God, help me to make wise choices so I don't have any regrets
when I'm older. I want to be committed to You and not dabble in
the empty pleasures of the world. Amen.*

*Then God blessed them and said, "Be fruitful and multiply.
Fill the earth and govern it. Reign over the fish in the sea,
the birds in the sky, and all the animals that
scurry along the ground."*
GENESIS 1:28 NLT

God let the first man, Adam, know what to do. Family was
important and so was hard work.

When people have a lot of free time they often do things
they regret. Work makes it easier to stay out of trouble.

In the 1880s, the authorities in Greensburg, Kansas, hired
a dozen men a day to dig a massive water well. The employees
earned fifty cents a day. The jobs were open to cowboys,
farmers, and those passing through. Today the well is a museum
and guests can walk down a spiral staircase into the hand-dug
well that is 109 feet deep.

The Big Well is just one example of the hard work that kept
men out of trouble and helped to provide for their families. Hard
work was one of the first things God told humankind to do. He
hasn't changed His mind.

*Dear God, You want me to work hard. The work I do can
bring me satisfaction, but it can bring You honor. Give me the
patience and the endurance needed to do whatever
work You send my way. Amen.*

UNDER PRESSURE

The temptations in your life are no different from what others experience. And God is faithful. He will not allow the temptation to be more than you can stand. When you are tempted, he will show you a way out so that you can endure.
1 CORINTHIANS 10:13 NLT

There's a big difference between temptation and trials. Many think they're the same. The first gives you a choice, but both give you an opportunity to trust God deeply.

Our enemy, Satan, uses temptations to try to convince us we don't really have to follow God's instructions. He wants us to fail. When we do fail, he's quick to suggest that God could never love someone who sins. He's lying.

Trials are struggles that seem too big to handle. This might be the loss of a job or home. It could be an impossible health issue.

God's Word says He gives us everything we need to resist temptation. We endure by following His instructions.

The same is never promised for trials. So next time you hear that God doesn't give you anything you can't handle, remember that He actually does. Sometimes the only one who can rescue us from the trials we face is God. If we could do it ourselves, we wouldn't need Him.

*Dear God, You've equipped me to resist temptation.
You can rescue me from the most difficult trials I'll face.
You've given gifts that can't be bought.
You must really love me. Thanks. Amen.*

We demolish arguments and every pretension that sets itself up against the knowledge of God, and we take captive every thought to make it obedient to Christ. And we will be ready to punish every act of disobedience, once your obedience is complete.
2 CORINTHIANS 10:5–6 NIV

Can you explain to others the reason you follow God? If someone asks you a question about your faith, could you answer?

There are a lot of confusing ideas out there, and no one seems willing to say there is an absolute truth. Most people will say something like, "You can't tell me what to believe." That's true, you can't. However, their lack of belief doesn't change the fact that Jesus said, "I am the way and the truth and the life. No one comes to the Father except through me" (John 14:6 NIV).

Dear God, You want me to discern whether what I hear is true when compared to the Bible or if it's something I should abandon with a warning to others. Help me listen to others, share what I know, and match their claims against Your Word. Amen.

How long must I struggle with anguish in my soul,
with sorrow in my heart every day?
PSALM 13:2 NLT

There's not much that feels worse than being alone. This isn't the spending-time-by-yourself alone, but the kind that believes no one cares enough about you to even think about you. This is the type of alone that not only collects negative thoughts, but rejects hope.

The book of Psalms showcases brilliant moments of worship, but also painful moments where the writer feels rejected and completely alone.

These verses in God's Word are intentional. We get a front row seat to some incredible pain. The writer talks about enemies, setbacks, and profound loneliness. A phrase that occurs throughout Psalms is, "How long?" The writer feels like the pain will never end. He wants hope, but hope is rare.

There are those who may think death is a good way to end the loneliness. If this ever crosses your mind, remember that when a psalm starts with "How long?" it continues by pointing to the hope found in the God who can answer the question.

Dear God, I never face struggles alone. You're my companion.
You know the way through and out of the loneliness I feel.
Suicide is a long-term decision for something that is usually
a short-term crisis. When I need help, let me find it.
When I need hope, let me always look to You. Amen.

NOT A SMALL SIN

Mean people spread mean gossip;
their words smart and burn.
PROVERBS 16:27 MSG

It doesn't take much effort to say something about someone that you have no proof is true. You could make it up or tell others something you heard.

If you wanted to know how lightbulbs were invented, you could make up a story or ask around and get a *maybe-that's-true* story. Here's a creative idea. Why not go to a qualified source to get your information? You might feel a little awkward if you've been telling people that a guy named Jimmy discovered the lightbulb hovering over him when he had his first good idea.

If that sounds ridiculous, so is gossip, and God tells us not to do it.

Gossip is a sin, and it's not a smaller sin in God's eyes than lying, cheating, stealing, or murder.

Even if the only sin ever committed was gossip, we'd still need the perfect sacrifice of Jesus to pay the price. Every sin is a big deal. God's forgiveness is a bigger deal. Obedience is our best response.

Dear God, there are a lot of things I should skip talking about. When I share stories that I've not been given permission to discuss, about someone who's never actually shared the story with me, then I'm essentially finding opportunity to point out the faults of others when I have no idea if what I'm saying is true. Help me stop the gossip. Amen.

VISUAL REMINDERS

"Always remember these commands I give you today. . . .
Talk about them when you sit at home and walk along the road,
when you lie down and when you get up. Write them down and
tie them to your hands as a sign. Tie them on your forehead to
remind you, and write them on your doors and gates."
DEUTERONOMY 6:6–9 NCV

I'm a huge fan of sticky notes. If I need a reminder about something important, I jot it on a note and post it where I'll see it—the bathroom mirror, the refrigerator, beside my bed, on my steering wheel, or even on the coffeepot. I'm literally surrounded by sticky notes.

Visible reminders are really great tools for helping us keep focused on what's important. That's why God told the Israelites to keep His commands by putting visual reminders in places they'd see frequently. You can do the same by writing scripture on notecards and posting them in your locker, around your mirror, on your wall in your bedroom, or even beside the toilet (a great time to take a minute to pray or meditate). So grab some notecards and get started today!

Father, I'm so thankful for Your Word and all the guidance,
encouragement, and comfort it brings me. As I place
scripture in visual places all around me, help me to
feel Your presence all day long. Amen.

A LEADER'S FIRST STEP

[Jesus said], "Among you it will be different.
Whoever wants to be a leader among you must be your servant,
and whoever wants to be first among you must become your
slave. For even the Son of Man came not to be served
but to serve others and to give his life as a ransom for many."
MATTHEW 20:26–28 NLT

There's more to being a boss than being bossy. When Christians lead, we should be different. We lead by example, which means we do so with a heart willing to show what a job well done looks like. We lead with an attitude of service.

If you think it seems unfair, consider this: "The Son of Man came not to be served, but to serve others." He's our example. There's another reason He came as a servant-leader. His mission was to rescue many by being a servant of all. That's why Jesus is the perfect Savior.

Dear God, life as a follower of Jesus is so different than
what I'm used to seeing. To have, I must give; and to lead,
I must serve. Help me understand that I always need to look
to the example of Your Son, Jesus, to see that serving
is the first step to leading. Amen.

RETIRING A REBELLIOUS HEART

An eye that disdains a father and despises a mother—
that eye will be plucked out by wild vultures
and consumed by young eagles.
PROVERBS 30:17 MSG

Sometimes God teaches lessons through word pictures. Today's verse offers a look at the end result of rebellion. What we see suggests that God takes rebellion seriously.

One of the problems with rebellion is it never seems to stop with the sin of rebellion, which can easily exist with dishonor, anger, selfish ambition, pride, and impatience.

Our families are given to us to help us learn to make good choices. When we insist on being rebellious instead of obedient, our parents may become less interested in guiding us. Stop listening and your family may stop speaking. The sad news is you will always wind up losing when rebellion becomes your typical response.

Rebellion always leads to regret. Admit the sin, accept God's forgiveness, apologize for your words and actions, and find a place to retire both a rebellious heart as well as the list of regrets that always stand ready to accuse.

Dear God, help me be willing to admit that I should ask for Your
help when I feel like rebelling. I don't want to live with regrets,
so help me honor those You tell me to honor. May I resist
rebelling against my family. May I refuse
to rebel against You. Amen.

THE STUBBORN, STONY HEART

[God said], "I will give you a new heart, and I will put a new spirit in you. I will take out your stony, stubborn heart and give you a tender, responsive heart."
EZEKIEL 36:26 NLT

Work with a shovel and your hands will become hard and rough. Play a guitar and your fingers develop a thicker layer of skin so they don't hurt when playing. This is a picture of what it's like to live with ongoing sin choices.

When you sin long enough, your heart develops a thick covering, making it less interested in God's plan. Imagine what that spiritual heart looks like after many years. Scars are evident along with dark and hard patches where sin has pounded away at principle and hope. This is the type of heart God is talking about.

This is the stubborn, stony sin heart that God can replace with a tender and responsive heart. It's true. God offers a spiritual heart replacement. This happens when we accept Jesus, but the potential of a newly hardened heart is something every Christian faces.

Maybe you understand what a hard heart looks like. Maybe it's time for something new.

Dear God, I want to respond to You in the right way. Some days I'm not sure I can. A hard heart makes it difficult to take anything seriously. Is it time to give me a new heart? I want to be responsive, and I need Your help. Amen.

FINDING TREASURE

Every part of Scripture is God-breathed and useful one way or another—showing us truth, exposing our rebellion, correcting our mistakes, training us to live God's way. Through the Word we are put together and shaped up for the tasks God has for us.
2 TIMOTHY 3:16–17 MSG

When we say that the Bible is *inerrant,* it means the Bible contains no errors. God inspired men over many centuries and locations to write His words. The Bible wasn't written in a single language or through one person. The Bible is a book of history and has been used to locate important artifacts. It is a book of poetry. Psalms represent this writing style perfectly. It contains love stories, battles, miracles, and instructions for living.

God's words in printed form are like finding treasure. We don't have to guess what God wants from us. We don't have to wonder what He provides for us. We can read that the God of the universe identifies with us, loves us, and has a plan for us.

We can trust His words, which are "God-breathed and useful. . .showing us truth. . .correcting our mistakes. . .[and] training us to live God's way."

We have His words. There's treasure here.

Dear God, thank You for never leaving me without direction. I have Your words and I have Your Spirit to help me learn and understand the many things You want me to know about You and the life You want me to live. Amen.

THE GRACE INVENTOR

> "For God so loved the world, that he gave his only Son,
> that whoever believes in him should not perish but have eternal
> life. For God did not send his Son into the world to condemn the
> world, but in order that the world might be saved through him."
> JOHN 3:16–17 ESV

God loves you. Salvation through His Son, Jesus, is the greatest gift humankind will ever know.

We may all be familiar with John 3:16, but it's the next verse that helps us understand that God is the inventor of grace. He could have sent each of us a list of law violations with a threat of what might happen to us if we don't change. He could have developed a huge prison system for lawbreakers (although all of us have broken His law—see Romans 3:23). He could even have destroyed the earth and started all over again. He could have, but He chose grace instead.

Verse 17 tells us that God didn't use the plan of salvation to initiate a secret agenda to condemn us.

It's easier to love someone who is for us—not against us.

Dear God, You provided an atmosphere where I could
identify with Jesus, trust Him to take care of me,
and view Him as worth following. Salvation is a free gift.
The only thing I have to do is trust (believe) in who You are
and what You can do. Thanks for accepting me. Amen.

ACCESSING OUR INTERNAL MEMORY BANK

I have stored up your word in my heart,
that I might not sin against you.
PSALM 119:11 ESV

Before there were banks or credit unions there were coffee cans and piggy banks. People would place coins and dollars inside and make a withdrawal when their need was the greatest. It was a pretty sad day when there was a need, but no money stored up.

When you take the time to memorize a Bible verse, you're intentionally storing it away for a future need. The more you *fill up* your memory bank the easier it'll be to make a withdrawal.

Memorizing God's Word helps us remember what He's said even when we're not near a Bible. Knowing His Word means it's less likely we'll question what God has said. We can use our internal hard drive to access God's truth so we can handle temptation, share God's truth anywhere, and remember the words when we need encouragement.

We don't memorize to earn gold stars, but to develop a sense of awe at who God is.

Dear God, You want me to store Your Words on the pages of my heart. For the benefit of those I share with, for my own benefit, and because I want to honor You, please help me make regular memory deposits filled with Your truth. Amen.

TRANSFORMED THROUGH OBEDIENCE

This is love: that we walk in obedience to his commands.
As you have heard from the beginning, his command
is that you walk in love.
2 JOHN 1:6 NIV

In the Old Testament there are dozens of laws. The most famous have been called the Ten Commandments (see Exodus 20). In the New Testament Jesus said the two greatest commandments had to do with how we love God and how we love others (see Mark 12:28–31).

If we're transformed from people who choose sin to people who choose God's plan through obedience then we probably need to understand how we get from one choice to the other.

Obedience is simply choosing to love. If we really love someone, we won't lie to them, steal from them, or say rude things to or about them. If we love God, we'll honor His name, take Him seriously, and serve Him well.

We're transformed when our choices are defined by love (see 1 Corinthians 13).

Our journey with God begins with multiple steps of loving obedience and ends with a transformation in the way we act, think, and live.

Dear God, You're very interested in my obedience. You give me all kinds of ways to be obedient through choices to love others. Help me start remembering that obedience is a life called to a transformation from mistrust to love. Amen.

Nevertheless, many even of the authorities believed in him,
but for fear of the Pharisees they did not confess it.
JOHN 12:42 ESV

I recently made some new friends who aren't Christians, and I found myself hiding my faith, afraid of their reaction once they learned I was a Christian. Would they still accept me? Or would they distance themselves from me, treating me like an outsider, judging me? So I kept quiet. But I couldn't hide my faith forever—it's too much a part of me. More importantly, I didn't want to. Whatever their reaction, I wanted to be true to myself and God.

Do you ever hide your faith because you fear people's reactions? Are you afraid your friends will make fun of you? Jesus endured humiliation to die for you. Will a certain group ostracize you? Jesus left heaven so you could be with Him. Do you crave the crowd's acceptance? More than anyone, Jesus—the Creator of the universe—wants you to be His friend.

Jesus is not ashamed of you. Don't be ashamed of Him.

Jesus, forgive me for the times I've denied You or hidden my faith
from others because I feared their reaction. Help me share
my faith openly and honestly. Amen.

For a child is born to us, a son is given to us. The government will rest on his shoulders. And he will be called: Wonderful Counselor, Mighty God, Everlasting Father, Prince of Peace. His government and its peace will never end. He will rule with fairness and justice from the throne of his ancestor David for all eternity.
ISAIAH 9:6–7 NLT

Bombs are launched from one nation to another. Crime in our communities plasters the local news. Feuding parents lead to divorce and broken families. All around us, there's so much pain and suffering and injustice. People try to promote peace, but can it really happen? With Jesus—yes!

Jesus came to establish peace—not only with Him, but with each other. Acceptance of His sacrifice on the cross brings peace between us and God. And following His ways promotes peace with those around us by forgiving, loving, and serving one another. Whether warring nations or warring parents disrupt our lives, the Prince of Peace has the power to bring harmony.

What personal or global situations need your prayers for peace today?

God, sometimes peace seems so impossible. The hate is too strong. The hurt is too much. But You are the God of the impossible. Please bring Your peace today. Help stop the anger and the bitterness and replace it with Your forgiveness and healing. Amen.

A MINIMIZED ME

*This is what the LORD says: "Don't let the wise boast
in their wisdom, or the powerful boast in their power,
or the rich boast in their riches."*
JEREMIAH 9:23 NLT

Have you been around people who can't wait to show the evidence of their brains, muscles, or money?

No one seems impressed if they have to be told how special and important those things make a person. Pride makes a bad coat. It covers you, but looks horrible.

When you're truly wise, others will notice without the need to buy a billboard proclaiming the fact. If you're rich, use it to help others. If you're powerful, use restraint to show God's love and mercy.

Humility means you simply do the right thing without looking for credit, without trying to get noticed, and without caring what other people think.

That's hard when you'd love to be recognized for a job well done. God notices what you do, and He's pleased when you let the praise for your work come from others.

*Dear God, Jesus came to earth and lived like one of us.
He was Your Son. He was something much more than one of us,
He came from heaven! His humble heart helps me understand
that when my priority is to honor You, then recognition
by others is simply a bonus. Amen.*

IT IS WELL

*"Peace I leave with you; my peace I give you.
I do not give to you as the world gives. Do not let
your hearts be troubled and do not be afraid."*
JOHN 14:27 NIV

Horatio Spafford famously wrote the hymn "It Is Well with My Soul." But do you know his story? A thriving lawyer in Chicago, he had wealth and prominence. But a series of tragedies stripped him of everything. His only son died of scarlet fever at the age of four. A year later, the Great Chicago Fire wiped out the city and all of Horatio's wealth. Two years later, all four of his remaining children died in a shipwreck. Sailing for England to join his wife, who survived the shipwreck, he passed the spot where his daughters were buried at sea. Upon seeing the sight, Horatio sat down and penned "It Is Well with My Soul." All his children—gone. His house—burned. But His soul—at peace.

Even in the face of tremendous heartache, Christ's peace anchored Horatio. No matter what happens, can you also sing, "Whatever my lot, Thou hast taught me to say, It is well, it is well with my soul"? Why or why not?

Jesus, I'm so thankful for Your peace and comfort, especially during tough times. Death and tragedy don't have to hurt so much because of the hope You give. Please give me peace and comfort today for the things that upset me. Amen.

How gracious he will be when you cry for help!
As soon as he hears, he will answer you. . . . Whether you turn
to the right or to the left, your ears will hear a voice
behind you, saying, "This is the way; walk in it."
ISAIAH 30:19, 21 NIV

Sometimes making decisions seems like playing hide-and-seek with God. He hides—and we have to seek! But Jesus always wants you to find Him.

You won't get very far in hide-and-seek if all you do is stand in one spot. You have to search. You can pray and pray and pray when you need God's direction, but you also have to get your move on. Take some action! Move a little to the left. Rats, a closed door. Okay, how about to the right? Oh, an open one! Okay, what's through here?

If you aren't sure which summer job to accept, pursue all your options until you feel God guiding you to the right one. Unsure what spring sport to play? Try out for soccer *and* track, and see which one brings you more joy and peace.

Finding God's will shouldn't remain an unsolved mystery. The magi followed a star. Moses saw a burning bush. Elijah heard a whisper. Look around you. What clues is God giving you?

Lord, thanks for always guiding me. Help me move in the right
direction by opening and closing doors and giving me
peace when I make the right decision. Amen.

LOVING THE HARD-TO-LIKE

*[Jesus said], "Love your enemies, do good to those who hate you,
bless those who curse you, pray for those who abuse you. . . .
And as you wish that others would do to you, do so to them."*
LUKE 6:27–28, 31 ESV

We come face-to-face with people who hate, curse, use, and
abuse, and are considered enemies. Shouldn't they be punished
for bad behavior?

Jesus told us to love bullies and those in training. That
doesn't mean we approve of their behavior, but showing God's
love to someone who is undeserving brings them face-to-face with
an unexpected gift. The impact can be life changing.

Our verses end with the Golden Rule. If you want love,
friendship, and kindness—demonstrate it, even to the hard-to-like.
God changed your heart. He can change theirs.

*Dear God, it's easy to want to get even with those who are rude.
At best I just hope to avoid mean people. You want more
from me. You want kindness where frustration usually exists.
You want love where anger is present. Help me readjust
my thinking to line up with Yours. Amen.*

All praise to God, the Father of our Lord Jesus Christ.
God is our merciful Father and the source of all comfort.
He comforts us in all our troubles so that we can comfort others.
When they are troubled, we will be able to give them
the same comfort God has given us.
2 CORINTHIANS 1:3–4 NLT

The Bible says, "In this world you will have trouble" (John 16:33 NIV). God promised that difficulties would be normal. That may sound like a promise we'd be happy to see God fail to keep. We don't like to worry, fear, or struggle. The good news is we don't have to.

God is described as merciful. He offers comfort whenever the struggles come. He may not shield us from trouble, but He does give us a place to rest in the middle of the trials we face.

In those times of testing we grow, we're stretched, and we learn a lot about ourselves and others. When God comforts us, it becomes our responsibility to comfort others and help them find God, the ultimate source of comfort.

We often ask why we have to go through difficulties, but if we accept that everyone struggles then we may ask the new question, "What do You want me to learn?"

Dear God, because You love us You provide comfort.
Because I love You I can show comfort to others.
Help me remember compassion demonstrates love. Amen.

TAKING THE SHAPE OF YOUR CHOICE

*As obedient children, let yourselves be pulled into a way
of life shaped by God's life, a life energetic and blazing
with holiness. God said, "I am holy; you be holy."*
1 PETER 1:14–16 MSG

Conforming is like placing your palm on a memory foam pillow.
The pillow quickly takes the shape of your hand. When you
decide to stop obeying God, you can quickly take the shape of
the many bad decisions you face every day. You *slip back into
those old grooves of evil.*

For the Christian, there is a better way. You no longer
have an excuse for making bad choices. God always offers
forgiveness, but He has always wanted us to grow up. He tells
us, "I am holy; you be holy."

That's wisdom from a God that knows it's easy for us to
make selfish decisions.

*Dear God, I need to be disciplined in my journey with You,
but that's part of growing up to serve You. Help me refuse
to be conformed to the shape of the easy decisions around
me. Help me break the mold and be used by You
to reshape the culture around me. Amen.*

GOOD CROP-BAD CROP

Don't be misled: No one makes a fool of God. What a person plants, he will harvest. The person who plants selfishness, ignoring the needs of others—ignoring God!—harvests a crop of weeds. All he'll have to show for his life is weeds! But the one who plants in response to God, letting God's Spirit do the growth work in him, harvests a crop of real life, eternal life.
GALATIANS 6:7–8 MSG

If life is a farm and we're farmers, then we're in the business of growing crops. If we don't plant good seed then weeds will grow.

A good crop has a positive impact on our lives and on the lives of others. We share love, hope, and kindness, and we harvest the same.

A bad crop is defined by its negative impact. When we express anger, violence, and hatred, we shouldn't be surprised when we don't gather a crop of joy.

If you think you can play along the fringes of a bad crop grown by others, you're likely to bring back bad seeds that overtake your crop.

Let God's Spirit clean out the weeds in your life and plant new seed. A harvest is coming. What's your life producing?

Dear God, every one of my actions today impacts my future. It takes time for any crop to grow, but there will come a time when everyone can see what type of seed I planted. Help me plant a crop that represents Your work in my life. Amen.

LOVE'S BASIC TRAINING

Love is patient, love is kind. It does not envy, it does not boast, it is not proud. It does not dishonor others, it is not self-seeking, it is not easily angered, it keeps no record of wrongs.
1 CORINTHIANS 13:4–5 NIV

The adults in your life have tried to teach you good manners for a reason. It's not just so you will be polite when someone visits or show respect for people who are older than you. The best reason is that when showing manners you are demonstrating what God describes as *love.*

Good manners means you will be kind, respectful, humble, honoring to others, calm, and patient. All of these are choices we make when it comes to love.

If you think manners are something that requires you to suppress personal rudeness until a person leaves, then you need to read the verses again. Manners are basic training for how to love your family, friends, strangers, and the girl you marry someday.

Manners aren't temporary restrictions; they are permanent guards that encourage us to love.

Dear God, what I say and how I say it are important to You. How I act and respond demonstrate whether I'm letting You change me for the better. Who I'm kind to and how unlimited I am with manners helps me learn important ways to show Your love to anyone. Help me honor people I don't even know through the choice to love—using manners. Amen.

*This means that anyone who belongs to Christ has become
a new person. The old life is gone; a new life has begun!*
2 CORINTHIANS 5:17 NLT

Ninety percent of sexually exploited women were abused
as children and fell through the cracks of society, landing in
prostitution. The US State Department estimates 100,000 children
(average age thirteen) enter sex trafficking *every year*. The sex
trade is a modern-day form of slavery where women and girls
are turned into property to be bought and sold.

Ninety-five percent of trafficked women say they want
out of their lifestyle, but they do not believe they can survive
doing anything else. New Friends New Life is a Christian
organization based in Dallas, Texas, that seeks to restore and
empower trafficked teen girls and sexually exploited women
and their children by providing access to education, job training,
temporary financial assistance, and counseling. Their mission is
to rehabilitate women, giving them new friends and a new life.

Learn more at www.newfriendsnewlife.org.

*Thank You, Father, for organizations that seek to restore abused
women and give them a new life. I pray that organizations like
these will continue to grow and provide help for all the hurting
women that want to leave the sex trade. Please give sex victims
courage to leave prostitution and start a new life. Amen.*

A DAY IS COMING

Therefore, with minds that are alert and fully sober,
set your hope on the grace to be brought to you
when Jesus Christ is revealed at his coming.
1 PETER 1:13 NIV

One day Jesus will come back. He will still be the Savior, but His coming means the start of something new. Earth isn't the end of His plan. He's created a place for each Christian in the place where He lives—heaven.

What happens here is only the beginning, but it is where the greatest decision about where we will spend eternity is made.

It takes faith to believe in a God we've never seen who lives in a place we've never been, but who has always existed, always will exist, and who created our world with nothing but the words He spoke.

Yet faith means we see proof of His existence in the air that we breathe, in the sun that rose this morning, in the food we eat, in the water we drink, in the friends we make, and in the family we love.

God wants us to take our faith seriously. He wants our minds, hearts, and lives locked into following Him so when He returns we'll be found faithful.

The best life is ahead.

Dear God, You don't want me to play games with my faith.
I shouldn't look at following You as the next big trend,
fad, or trial offer. You're God. Help me always
understand the need to follow You. Amen.

*Hallelujah! Praise God in his holy house of worship,
praise him under the open skies; Praise him for his acts
of power, praise him for his magnificent greatness. . . .
Let every living, breathing creature praise GOD! Hallelujah!*
PSALM 150:1–2, 6 MSG

We're told to praise God, but what does that mean? In today's culture we usually think of a church service or outdoor festival where people sing songs to and about God. There are praise bands, praise songs, and praise gatherings, but is this all there is to praise?

Music does seem to be one of the most-used methods to praise God, but to praise means more than singing songs. To praise God can look like an awards ceremony where you think of all the reasons God deserves your trust and faith. Praise can be a bit like boasting by telling others how amazing God is. Praise can be a session of gratitude where you thank God personally for the many gifts He has given.

*Dear God, when I praise You, I'm letting You know I understand
You made everything, gave everything, and deserve everything
I've got—and I agree that You're more than worthy of all the
gratitude I can ever give. You're beyond awesome. Amen.*

EVERY MOMENT POTENTIAL

You saw me before I was born. Every day of my life
was recorded in your book. Every moment was laid
out before a single day had passed.
PSALM 139:16 NLT

Do you ever wonder if you have any real potential? You look at things other guys are good at and you say, "That's just not me." It's easy to feel like you don't measure up.

Welcome to a better understanding of potential. The psalmist said that before your family welcomed you into the world God had a record of every day of your life. Not just the highlights, but every moment.

The psalmist said, "You made all the delicate, inner parts of my body and knit me together in my mother's womb" (Psalm 139:13).

God made you in His image, offers a plan and hope for your future, and loved you enough to redeem you from the price of accumulated sin. Do you have potential? The answer is found in everything God has done to demonstrate the unique way He handcrafted you—yes!

Dear God, Your Word reminds me I was created
for a purpose, and my purpose may be different than
that of anyone else. My potential rests in You. You have urged
me to become what You made me to be. Help me learn
what that is and be ready to grow. Amen.

*LORD, rescue me from evil people; protect me
from cruel people who make evil plans.*
PSALM 140:1–2 NCV

Human sex trafficking has become *the* human rights issue of today. According to the FBI, it's the fastest growing business in organized crime. The majority of sex trafficking happens in other countries, but did you know that around 300,000 American youths are at risk for becoming victims and an untold number have already been taken for trafficking? Girls between the ages of twelve and fourteen are forced into prostitution, and even boys between the ages of eleven and thirteen are trafficked in the United States. Victims are sold to traffickers, locked up for weeks or months, drugged, terrorized, and raped. Victims become so afraid, they don't fight and they won't escape, even when presented with an opportunity. Once they are prostituted, the average victim is forced to have sex twenty to forty-eight times a day.

Human trafficking isn't just an international problem—it's a local one. Trafficking happens in all fifty states, 365 days a year.

With your parents' permission, you can learn more about human trafficking at www.polarisproject.org.

Jesus, please rescue sex trafficking victims, and help them find healing. Please guide law enforcement to recognize where trafficking is happening and shut it down. And please help awareness to spread so trafficking can be prevented and better reported to the authorities. Amen.

PERSONAL FAITH

*God had special plans for me and set me apart for his work
even before I was born. He called me through his grace
and showed his son to me so that I might tell the Good
News about him to those who are not Jewish.*
GALATIANS 1:15–16 NCV

Paul was the model Jew. He grew up memorizing scripture,
attending synagogue every week, and participating in Jewish
festivals. He did everything right! But one day he met Jesus face-
to-face, and his whole life changed.

Many teens have the same background as Paul. They grew
up in Christian homes, attending church and youth group every
week, memorizing scripture, and participating in Christian
holidays. But they haven't met Jesus face-to-face.

Our faith isn't just a bunch of rules and beliefs passed down
from our parents and grandparents; it's a personal encounter
with a living God. Have you had a life-changing experience with
Jesus Christ, or are you just going through the motions, leaning
on your parents' faith?

*Jesus, I want to know You—truly know You. Not just learn
about You and "do the right things." I want to experience
You like Paul did. Please show Yourself to me so that I can
know You personally and the plans You have for me. Amen.*

MOTIVATION: A STAMP OF APPROVAL

*Stand your ground. And don't hold back. Throw yourselves
into the work of the Master, confident that nothing
you do for him is a waste of time or effort.*
1 CORINTHIANS 15:58 MSG

Do you ever have those mornings that just don't go right? You
don't want to get out of bed, you have zero motivation, and
yet you hope things change. You think becoming an adult and
getting a job you actually want will make the difference.

What if this is the wrong perspective? What if *everything*
you do is viewed as the work of God? What if nothing you do
for God is a waste of time?

As Christians our employer is God. He makes sure we're
taken care of now and when we get to heaven. Because we
serve Him we can endure any work we encounter, but we can
also be content knowing that we've done our best for Him.

While work is important, it's the motivation to do the work
that's the key to contentment. Work is a tool we use to honor
God. Seeking to honor God is what can motivate us to do the
work well.

*Dear God, whenever I begin to feel like I would rather do
anything but the work I have to do right now help me remember I
work for You. You created everything and notice when
I do something right. Help me remember this the next time
I can't find the motivation to serve You well. Amen.*

FREE TO SERVE

For you have been called to live in freedom, my brothers and sisters. But don't use your freedom to satisfy your sinful nature. Instead, use your freedom to serve one another in love.
GALATIANS 5:13 NLT

You are free to love. You are free to serve. You are free to be what God made you to be.

The freedom God gives isn't bent toward selfishness, but bent toward seeing freedom as a way to bless others.

Every trait that God wants to develop in our lives has the choice to love at its center. He calls this love *freedom*.

When we serve others, we're demonstrating the truth of our choice to love. After all, who willingly serves the needs of others if they don't really care for them?

Service requires humility because you're not looking out for the things you want, but for the needs of others. Sometimes the people you serve are people you don't even know. However, when you know the individual you serve, it creates the opportunity to view others as more important than you.

Perhaps one of the greatest freedoms we have is freedom from selfishness.

Dear God, when I think of freedom I think of doing what I want to do, but Your words say that freedom is something different. You want me to be freed from self and free to share life with others. Help me see freedom as never having to apologize for serving others in Your name. Amen.

VENDING MACHINE CHRISTIANITY?

My purpose in writing is simply this: that you who believe in God's Son will know beyond the shadow of a doubt that you have eternal life, the reality and not the illusion. And how bold and free we then become in his presence, freely asking according to his will, sure that he's listening. And if we're confident that he's listening, we know that what we've asked for is as good as ours.
1 JOHN 5:13–15 MSG

God has never been a vending machine. Does that sound like an odd statement? Sometimes we treat Him as if all we need to do is pay the price of a prayer and He'll *have* to answer our request in the way we want it answered.

Since God knows everything, He's aware of what's good for us and what will cause us harm. Wouldn't God be irresponsible if He let us have things He knew would harm us?

When we invite God to fuse His will with our request, the answer we receive will be perfect. Does that mean God will give us what we want? It means we learn to desire God's will over our requests.

Dear God, since You know much more than I do, help me always ask for Your best. I want Your will even when I think I know what I would like. Help me remember that when I leave the decision to You, I'll always get something much better than I planned. Amen.

MY WILL FOR YOUR WAY

You will show me the way of life, granting me the joy of your
presence and the pleasures of living with you forever.
PSALM 16:11 NLT

It's possible to think that if God is all you have then you don't really have much. Some people think it's like choosing a library over a roller coaster. They feel that God just isn't exciting enough to allow Him to influence every part of their life. What if they spend time with God and miss out on something fun?

Surrendering to God means your perspective will change. You'll discover a secret that will surprise you. Every amazing experience you've ever had won't satisfy you the way God can. Every experience has a beginning and end. You'll get tired of each new experience. God always comes through.

God invites us to really live life with Him. That life comes with joy-filled satisfaction, encouraging us to put everything else lower on our priority list. Experiences can make us happy, but only God can bring joy, and in His presence you'll always find a greater satisfaction you didn't know was possible.

Dear God, You want me to fully realize that I could never have
a greater life than the one I can have as Your child.
No matter what I could ever try, it is only a small thing
compared to knowing You. Help me seek and find satisfaction
in You. Help me surrender my will for Your way. Amen.

GROWING FAITH

*You must learn to endure everything, so that you will be
completely mature and not lacking in anything.*
JAMES 1:4 CEV

Nobody *likes* to suffer. Even if you're a committed athlete, there
are some days you just don't want to practice—especially if
practice is so hard it makes you vomit! But we recognize that
the training, the suffering, matures us—it makes us better. We're
stronger and more skilled, sharper and more in control.

You can't mature into a champion athlete by sitting on the
couch!

Our spiritual life is the same. A strong, committed faith in
God doesn't just happen. It has to grow. God allows trouble
to come into our life so that He can train us and mature our
faith. The valley—not the mountaintop—is where God makes us
stronger.

What struggles are you facing right now? What do you think
God is teaching you? How is your faith growing?

*Lord, life is not fun right now. It actually really hurts.
It's hard to find any joy in all this, but I do find comfort in You.
You've been really close during this time, and I do feel
You growing me. So thank You for this experience
and deepening my faith in You. Amen.*

> *"Put on the full armor of God, so that when the day
> of evil comes, you may be able to stand your ground,
> and after you have done everything, to stand."*
> EPHESIANS 6:13 NIV

Quitting seems easy. You struggle with basketball because
it requires effort and a commitment to learn the rules. You
participate in band, but the shoulder harness on the drums hurts.
You take guitar lessons, but you want to set it aside because
something else catches your attention.

Some commitments should be set aside because they aren't
compatible with your talent or personality. Other commitments
are set aside because you just aren't as engaged as you thought.

The Christian life is designed to be a forever commitment.
God gives us tools He refers to as *armor* so that when we face
our spiritual enemy we can take a stand. We are in a spiritual
war and every tool God gives us is designed to resist the enemy.
If we quit, turn our back, and run away, we expose areas where
the adversary can wound us. When you've done all you can
do to quit, God offers full commitment to help you through His
command to "Stand firm."

*Dear God, You want me to honor commitments.
That means when I promise my family I'll do something
they can expect me to do it. It also means that when I follow You I
follow even when it's hard. Help me serve You with
the full dedication and backing of Your love. Amen.*

BAD DAYS CLEAR OUR VISION

*Consider it a sheer gift, friends, when tests and challenges
come at you from all sides. You know that under pressure,
your faith-life is forced into the open and shows its true colors.*
JAMES 1:2–3 MSG

Have you ever thought of a bad day as a gift? What if days like
this exist to provide a better picture of what's really important?

It can be easy to think that the most important thing in life is
to have days without stress, worry, and pain. The trouble is we
often forget God when things are good.

We live in a world where it's easy for people to make bad
choices. Bad things often happen just because we live in a world
where people sin. Our lives and the sin of humanity will clash
from time to time. That's when we remember why God is so
important.

The pressure of bad days can help us bring our faith out of
hiding and prove that we really trust God.

*Dear God, sometimes bad days help shift my focus back
to You. When bad things happen, I remember You.
That doesn't mean You make things bad so I'll notice,
but today I am noticing, and I'm grateful. Amen.*

ULTIMATE POSSESSION

In heaven I have only you, and on this earth you
are all I want. My body and mind may fail,
but you are my strength and my choice forever.
PSALM 73:25–26 CEV

Your house is on fire, and you only have *one* thing you can save from being burned to ashes—what would you grab? No cheesy answers like your Bible or your pillow. But seriously, what would you be absolutely devastated to lose?

The answer to this question reveals your ultimate possessions in life. What would happen if it were destroyed? Why is it so special? Is the value sentimental or monetary?

Chances are what you grabbed isn't something you could take to heaven with you. You never see a U-Haul following a funeral procession so the person who died can be buried with all his belongings.

So what really matters? Is it stuff? People's opinions of us? How well we perform?

It all really boils down to God. He's our ultimate possession—the one thing we can never lose.

What do you fear losing? What possessions do you cling to? What status are you chasing? What do you need to surrender to God in order for Him to be the ultimate desire of your heart?

God, it's so easy to chase after unimportant things. To guard my
stuff and not want to share it. But You are what's truly lasting and
most important. I surrender everything to You. Amen.

ZIP THE LIP!

Blessing and cursing come pouring out of the same mouth. Surely, my brothers and sisters, this is not right! Does a spring of water bubble out with both fresh water and bitter water?
JAMES 3:10–11 NLT

Jeremy came from a very poor family. Because he was smelly, overweight, and obnoxious, kids always made fun of him and picked on him before youth group started. Then the youth pastor would get the night rolling, and the same mouths that had mocked Jeremy switched to praising God.

When you make fun of others, you are essentially making fun of God because we are all made in His image. When you use your words to hurt or mock others, you are hurting and mocking God. Bitter saltwater added to a glass of freshwater ruins the whole glass. Similarly, your praises to God are empty if you're speaking badly of others.

The next time you're tempted to lash out or make a biting remark, zip the lip! If you mess up and say things you shouldn't, make it right. Ask for God's forgiveness and the other person's. Use your words to be an instrument of blessing, not destruction.

God, help me honor You with my words—not just in praises, but in how I speak to others. Amen.

I'LL MAKE CHANGES TOMORROW

*You don't know the first thing about tomorrow.
You're nothing but a wisp of fog, catching
a brief bit of sun before disappearing.*
JAMES 4:14 MSG

How much time do you spend with God? This book offers three minutes a day or twenty-one minutes a week. If you spent time here every day you might dedicate an hour and a half by the end of a month. For the purpose of comparison, how much time do you spend with family? How about in after-school activities? How much time do you spend on entertainment (TV, computer, phone, video games, etc.)? Do your answers make 3 minutes seem like a small investment?

It's easy to live as if tomorrow is promised. You could easily promise that tomorrow you'll spend more time with God, family, and friends. It's easy to make decisions about what you know is important as long as you can say those changes will be made in the future.

You don't have a promise of a future *day of change*. However, you can make sure that the time you spend today is used to honor God and to improve your understanding of His plan.

Dear God, I'm grateful I've spent this time with You. Help me understand that time is an investment and that some activities don't have the ability to improve the plans You've had for me since before I was born. Amen.

TAMING THE TONGUE

All kinds of animals, birds, reptiles and sea creatures are being tamed and have been tamed by mankind, but no human being can tame the tongue. It is a restless evil, full of deadly poison.
JAMES 3:7–8 NIV

Tongue twisters drive me nuts! My mind knows what it *should* say, but my mouth pops out the wrong thing! But with enough practice (and going slowly enough!), I can recite tongue twisters correctly.

Taming our words can seem an impossible task. You know what you *should* say, but out pops mean and unkind things. But good news! We don't have to tackle this impossible task on our own. The Holy Spirit will help you. So pay attention to His nudges, and the more you practice controlling your words, the easier it will become.

How much control do you use when speaking? Do you try to filter your words, or do you just let them fly without thought? Do you find yourself easily criticizing, or do you like to encourage? In what way do you most need to work on taming your tongue?

Holy Spirit, please show me how I need to watch my words. Convict me when I'm saying things I shouldn't, and help me practice restraint—holding in the damaging things I want to say. Help me not to criticize and gossip, but to lift up and encourage. Amen.

LOVE PREVAILS

If we confess our sins, he is faithful and just and will forgive us our sins and purify us from all unrighteousness.
1 JOHN 1:9 NIV

What's your weakness? What do you give in to? What mistake do you repeatedly make?

We all have weaknesses. We all sin. But it's our response to sin that's key. Do you retreat from God because you enjoy the sin so much you'd rather wallow in it than walk away from it? Do you beat yourself up with guilt and come up with strategies on how it's never going to happen again? Do you hide it from the world and act like everything is fine, but find yourself buried with shame? Do you go out and have fun because if you forget about it, you'll feel better?

There is never a time you'll feel more unworthy to approach God, to sit in your shame and ask for forgiveness, than when you make a mistake. But when weakness wins, love prevails. God's love for you is not dependent on who you are, what you have to offer, or how "good" you are. God loves you. Period.

God's love is undeserved and beyond what you could pay for it. But it's there, for you, ready and available to experience, if you confess your sins.

*God, I've messed up—again. Please forgive me.
I feel so unworthy, so undeserving. Thank You for revealing
to me the depth of Your grace. Amen.*

*Then Jesus said, "Come to me, all of you who are weary
and carry heavy burdens, and I will give you rest. Take my yoke
upon you. Let me teach you, because I am humble and gentle
at heart, and you will find rest for your souls. For my yoke
is easy to bear, and the burden I give you is light."*
MATTHEW 11:28–30 NLT

If you believe you should say yes to every opportunity, you need
to understand that God has a better plan.

God offers to take your burden and replace it with a
manageable load. You could complete many good things, but
even good things can keep you away from God's best.

You're never asked to stop serving God, but there are times
when there's a limit to what you can do if you also want to do
what God has planned for you. Not everything you're asked to
do is God's plan for you. Pray, seek wisdom from trusted adults,
and make a decision that keeps you from overwhelming stress
and frustration.

*Dear God, You want me to serve others, but You also want me to
learn from You. In order to do both there may be times I need to
say no. Help me understand when that word is necessary. Amen.*

PERMISSION TO TURN YOUR BACK

Repent of your sins and turn to God,
so that your sins may be wiped away.
ACTS 3:19 NLT

It doesn't take much skill to sin, and it only gets easier.

Doing the wrong thing can seem empowering. Wearing the wardrobe of a rebel can appear to offer independence, but it never does.

The choice to sin is actually inviting our enemy to influence future decisions.

God knows the end result of sin is death, which is why He gives us access to life.

We're restored in our relationship with God when we turn from the easy choice to sin to the life-affirming choice to obey. Repentance requires turning away from the choice to sin.

Sometimes we want to be forgiven, but we don't want to stop making the same sinful choice. We ask God to forgive, but keep looking at and entertaining the same sinful choices.

The choice to turn away can seem hard. You have an emotional attachment to sin. God wants to change your mind. Repentance is your positive response to His desire to restore you to life.

Dear God, there are times I don't want to do the right thing. This is a bad place for me to be, and You've always offered a way out. You offer forgiveness, but You want me to turn my back on the easy choice and follow You. Help me listen for Your voice, read Your Words, and follow Your plan. Amen.

GOD AS FATHER

"I am the Alpha and the Omega," says the Lord God,
"who is, and who was, and who is to come, the Almighty."
REVELATION 1:8 NIV

When we think of God as our Father, many times we naturally compare Him to our own father. But our earthly fathers aren't perfect, and that can create misperceptions about God. So what does the Bible say Father God is like?

He is the creator of everything (see Acts 17:24–29) and the sovereign ruler of all nations (see 1 Timothy 6:15). He is a holy judge who deserves respect and reverence (see 1 Peter 1:15–17; Ephesians 2:1–3). He demands justice for our sins, but also provides loving mercy through offering His own Son to take our punishment (see Romans 3:24–26). He loves us and takes pleasure in us and lavishes us with His blessings (see Ephesians 1:3–14). He is faithful (see 1 Corinthians 1:9) and passionate about restoring our relationship with Him (see John 3:16).

What does the term *Father* mean to you? How much does your relationship with your earthly father affect your relationship with your heavenly Father? Is your view of God unbalanced? After learning what the Bible says about God as Father, how does your perception of Him need to change?

Father God, Your role as holy judge makes me approach
You with reverent respect. But Your compassion, mercy,
and love overwhelm me. You are mighty and powerful,
yet You love fervently. Thank You for loving me! Amen.

GOD AS SON

Christ is the visible image of the invisible God. He existed before anything was created and is supreme over all creation.
COLOSSIANS 1:15 NLT

Praise Jesus! Without Him, we would not have a complete picture of God. As part of the Trinity, Jesus existed before Creation and was fully God while also becoming fully human (see Philippians 2:6–11). But Jesus' role is different from the Father's.

While the Father is the author of all creation, He created through Jesus and Jesus sustains all life (see John 1:3; Colossians 1:16–17; Hebrews 1:2–3). Therefore, Jesus is supreme over all creation (see Colossians 1:15, 18; Hebrews 1:6). Jesus is Emmanuel, "God with us" (see Matthew 1:23), and the forgiver of sin (see Matthew 9:2; Luke 7:48; John 3:18).

The holiness of the Father keeps Him separate from us. We cannot see His face and live (see Exodus 33:20–23). But in His grace and mercy, God sent His Son so that we may see the face of God and receive the forgiveness of our sins. God is no longer separate from us, but through Jesus (Emmanuel!) God is now among us and we can truly know Him. That is definitely worth some praise!

Jesus, wow! You are so awesome! You created everything and sustain the workings of the universe. You became human so God could dwell among us and so we could be forgiven and restored to the Father. Thank You, God, for revealing Yourself to us! Amen.

GOD AS HOLY SPIRIT

*"But I will send you the Advocate—the Spirit of truth. He will
come to you from the Father and will testify all about me."*
JOHN 15:26 NLT

Of all the members of the Trinity, the Holy Spirit causes the most
controversy among Christians. Some completely overlook Him
and minimize His power and presence. Others overemphasize
the power of the Holy Spirit and place Him in a position of
prominence over the Father and the Son. What does scripture
say about this third member of the Trinity?

Jesus sent the Holy Spirit so we wouldn't be left as orphans
when He ascended to heaven (see John 14:18). Now God is
not just *with* us, but *in* us (see John 14:17; Romans 8:11; 1
Corinthians 6:19)! As our advocate, He comforts, encourages,
and counsels us (see Acts 9:31; John 14:16, 15:26). When we
don't know how to pray, the Holy Spirit prays for us (see Romans
8:26). He identifies us as God's children, guaranteeing our
eternal salvation (see Ephesians 4:30).

Through the Holy Spirit, God's presence is with us all the
time, teaching us, guiding us, convicting us, and encouraging us.
Jesus revealed God to us, and now the Holy Spirit allows God to
live inside us!

*Holy Spirit, thank You for never leaving me. I'm so glad You
remain in me, guiding me, counseling me, and encouraging me.
Continue to change me and make me more like Jesus. Amen.*

THE ANSWER TO YOUR QUESTION

*It you need wisdom, ask our generous God, and he will
give it to you. He will not rebuke you for asking.*
JAMES 1:5 NLT

Some decisions are easy. If you're offered two different fruits,
for instance, and you have a preference, then you grab your
favorite. If a friend asks you to steal something, you don't have
to think about it long. You leave the item there and carefully
consider the relationship you have with your friend.

As you grow up there are more questions. What college will
you choose? What girl will you marry? Should you buy a sports
car or a minivan?

Today's tough questions have to do with friends, character,
integrity, and trying to understand which of your choices is good
and which is best.

Take those choices to God and ask for wisdom. He's
generous and will provide an answer—even if it's not the one
you wanted. God doesn't just tell us what we want to hear. He
tells us what we need to hear. Always start looking for answers in
the Bible. He already knew you would ask.

*Dear God, it's good to know that I serve a God who wants the
best for me. It's an awesome thing that You never keep wisdom
away from me. All I have to do is ask. Help me to never forget
this step. Help me keep looking for Your solutions in the words
You've placed in the Bible. Amen.*

HOW DIFFERENT ARE YOU?

Now the works of the flesh are evident: sexual immorality, impurity, sensuality, idolatry, sorcery, enmity, strife, jealousy, fits of anger, rivalries, dissensions, divisions, envy, drunkenness, orgies, and things like these. I warn you, as I warned you before, that those who do such things will not inherit the kingdom of God. But the fruit of the Spirit is love, joy, peace, patience, kindness, goodness, faithfulness, gentleness, self-control; against such things there is no law.
GALATIANS 5:19–23 ESV

In this passage, Paul strongly contrasts the sinful nature with the fruit of the Spirit. Everyone can tell the difference between hatred and love, rage and kindness, getting drunk and having self-control. When we become "new creations" (see 2 Corinthians 5:17) in Christ, the sinful nature should disappear more and more while the fruit of the Spirit grows more evident. Just as the fruit of the Spirit contrasts sharply with the deeds of the sinful nature, Christians should stand out in the world.

Read over today's scripture again. What descriptions from the sinful nature especially stand out to you? What fruit of the Spirit do you see in your life? Which ones need to become more evident?

*Ouch, God. I'm still letting my sinful self rule by _____.
Please forgive me and work in my heart and life to be more
_____. As You transform my life, I pray that
I would sharply contrast the world in my behavior
so others can see You in me. Amen.*

BURNED OUT

*"If you are tired from carrying heavy burdens,
come to me and I will give you rest."*
MATTHEW 11:28 CEV

Sometimes do you ever just feel. . .burned out? Out of gas? The homework, the practices, the social obligations, running here, running there. You just want to drop into bed, pull the covers over your head, and sleep for a whole weekend.

Feeling burned out is a good sign that you need rest—that you're carrying too much by yourself. When we're accelerating through life on our own gas, we'll quickly putter out. We need to spend time refueling with God. Even Jesus withdrew from His busy ministry to spend time resting and refueling with the Father. Luke 5:16 says, "But Jesus would often go to some place where he could be alone and pray" (CEV). Did you catch that? Jesus *often* sought time alone.

How often do you seek downtime to be alone and spiritually refreshed? If you need some gas, some pep in your step, be sure to make a pit stop and drop your burdens at Jesus' feet. He'll refill your tank and give you the strength and energy you need to face your day.

Jesus, I'm so tired. I haven't been very good about coming to You for encouragement and refreshment. I spend my down time zoning out in front of the TV or on my phone, but that doesn't really refill my spirit. Help me turn to You for the rest I really need. Amen.

FRIEND INVESTMENTS

*Become wise by walking with the wise; hang out with fools
and watch your life fall to pieces.*
PROVERBS 13:20 MSG

If someone shows an interest in the things you're interested in,
should that be enough to indicate he or she will be a good
friend? Well, it's a start.

God knew the friends we have tend to help or hurt us the
more time we spend with them. For instance, if you have friends
that love Jesus, work hard, have good manners, and maintain
a great sense of humor, you might find yourself encouraged to
be more like them. If you have a friend that has no interest in
God, gets other people to do his work, doesn't respond well
to authority, and is extremely sarcastic, then becoming like that
person doesn't sound like such a great idea.

We become more like the person God designed us to be
when we invest time in friendships that encourage us in good
things. When we hang out with those who insist on doing things
that get them into trouble, it's entirely possible we will become
more like them than the men God wants us to be.

*Dear God, choosing friends is something You take seriously.
When I choose a friend who doesn't want to follow You it
becomes easier for me to think my commitment to You
might have been the wrong decision. Good friends bring out
the best. Help me find that kind of friend. Amen.*

SACRIFICE OF PRAISE

Thank the LORD because he is good. His love continues forever.
PSALM 118:1 NCV

During church, we often approach worship the same way we approach the sermon: What can I get out of it? If we don't walk away feeling spiritually encouraged and refreshed after our time of singing, we feel like the effort was a waste. But worship isn't for *us*. It's for *God*. We worship Him because He deserves our praise.

Worship is like writing thank-you notes. You don't write thank-yous to make *yourself* feel better; you write them to express honest and genuine thanks for a gift you've received. You may not feel like sitting down and writing a note, but you do anyway because the person deserves your acknowledgment and appreciation.

Some days it's easier to praise God than others. Some days we feel really close to Him, and some days offering any praise or thanks feels like it's vanishing into a void. Regardless of our feelings, we need to participate in worship and genuinely thank God for His goodness, love, and blessings in our life.

Instead of spending most of your prayer time today making requests of God, spend your time thanking Him and praising Him for who He is and for what He's done for you.

Lord, You are so good. You continually surprise me with loving gifts, and You're so faithful to provide—every time. I praise You for being sovereign and wise, for being just but merciful. Amen.

BURDEN OF GUILT

Day and night your hand of discipline was heavy on me.
My strength evaporated like water in the summer heat.
Finally, I confessed all my sins to you and stopped trying to hide
my guilt. I said to myself, "I will confess my rebellion to
the LORD." And you forgave me! All my guilt is gone.
PSALM 32:4–5 NLT

A new school year began, and I found myself hanging out with a new crowd of people. They weren't Christians, and I started making small compromises—suddenly doing and saying things I would never normally say and do. I knew it was wrong; I felt guilt immediately. But I shoved it down and kept changing my behavior to fit in with these new friends.

But guilt and conviction never go away. No matter how much you try to ignore it, you still feel it. It weighs on you. It chips away at your joy and happiness until all you feel is the strain. I was so miserable I finally confessed my rebellion to God. A weight finally lifted off my spirit, and I felt free!

It wasn't easy facing the rejection of my new friends once I stopped mimicking their lifestyle, but it was worth it. I was free from guilt, and the joy and peace of being right with God far outweighed the temporary, destructive friendships I'd made.

Thank You, Lord, for convicting me and not leaving
me alone until I'm right with You. Amen.

LOVING THE LOVELESS

The king will answer, "Whenever you did it for any of my people,
no matter how unimportant they seemed, you did it for me."
MATTHEW 25:40 CEV

We all prefer to stay in our comfort zone and relate with those
who are like us or who we want to be like. But Jesus tells us
that when we love others who are in need, we're serving and
giving directly to Jesus. Who do you pass every day in the halls
at school or in your neighborhood that could use some love and
help? How can you reach out to them? Could you befriend the
friendless? Buy supplies for someone who needs them? Do you
own clothes you don't wear that you could donate?

Whether you hang with a tight group of friends or find
yourself wishing you had more, today's verse applies to you.
Don't be so cozy in your friendships that you overlook or exclude
others who desperately need a friend. If you're looking for more
friends, reach out in friendship to someone you may normally
ignore. There's no better way to love Jesus than by loving the
loveless or those easily overlooked.

God, open my eyes to the people around me who need Your love
today. Show me how I can serve You by serving the overlooked
and "unimportant" people I see every day. Amen.

A TROUBLEMAKER'S SMALL QUESTIONS

Watch out for people who cause divisions and upset people's faith by teaching things contrary to what you have been taught. Stay away from them.
ROMANS 16:17 NLT

Asking good questions is a sign of a great mind. You want to learn because truth is important to you. Troublemakers *also* ask questions, but they ask questions in a way that encourages doubt about truth. You know God loves you, but a troublemaker might say, "Does God really love you?" If they want you to do something you know is wrong they might say, "How will your parents find out? They won't hear it from me."

The questions can be bold and confrontational, but usually there are many smaller questions that encourage little changes in how we view truth.

The question of a troublemaker never leads to an increased connection to God's truth. These questions always lead to distrust and a belief that no one can know the real truth about God and what He wants. If this is where you find yourself, please remember God gave us His words in the Bible. That's where truth lives.

Dear God, You are the author of truth. You created laws that allow humankind to exist and thrive. You gave us laws that help us grow a relationship with You. You also say that your truth brings freedom. Help me keep the freedom of truth close. Amen.

KIND WORDS

*Kind words are like honey—they cheer you up
and make you feel strong.*
PROVERBS 16:24 CEV

It's not hard to say hurtful things—especially behind someone's back or by posting something online or in a text. It's even easier to be mean and hurtful when someone has been a jerk to you. Why be nice when they started it? But what comes out of your mouth shows what's inside your heart. If hurtful and hateful speech pours out, what does that say about the condition of your heart?

Kind words spread like honey—nourishing the malnourished and refreshing the soul. When kindness from your heart genuinely comes out in kind words *to* others and *about* others, not only will your words refresh people's hungry souls, but you'll feel better, too, for not playing dirty with anger and gossip. Honey is sweet to the taste and healthy for the body. Likewise, kind words benefit others as well as those who use them.

Whose actions tempt you to speak hurtful words—a sibling, parent, friend? How can you speak encouragement to them? What words would show them kindness?

Lord, when I'm angry, please help me to calm myself down before saying mean or hurtful things. Help me not to get involved with gossip. Please change my heart and make it pure so I can genuinely love and speak kind words to others. Amen.

CRUSHING THE HOPE CANDLE

*Don't push your way to the front; don't sweet-talk your way
to the top. Put yourself aside, and help others get ahead.
Don't be obsessed with getting your own advantage.
Forget yourselves long enough to lend a helping hand.*
PHILIPPIANS 2:4 MSG

The Bible defines *selfish ambition* as the "works of the flesh." This is the kind of ambition that isn't satisfied with following personal dreams for a better future. It's the kind of ambition that throws a party when successfully crushing the dreams of others.

These individuals may look like bullies or work behind the scenes to set someone else up for failure. They have their own agenda and they enlist anyone they can to crush the flickering hope candle in the hearts of others.

These individuals make poor friends, but God's Word reminds us in bold language that He wants us to act differently. We should be humble enough to actually help someone achieve their dreams. We shouldn't manipulate circumstances to gain an advantage. We shouldn't think about ourselves at all. Think about people around you today. What can you do to help them reach a good goal?

*Dear God, when I'm selfishly ambitious I become ruthless in
getting my own way. You call this the work of the flesh because
it isn't something You would do. Sometimes You let us have our
way. It always ends badly. Help me forget myself "long
enough to lend a helping hand." Amen.*

Pile your troubles on God's shoulders—
he'll carry your load, he'll help you out.
PSALM 55:22 MSG

How much is too much? How busy is too busy? The answer is different for each person, but knowing your limits is helpful. You can borrow trouble by staying too busy or trying to take on too much.

The worst thing you can do is refuse God's help. He'll take as much stress and anxiety as you're willing to give. He'll never turn you away saying, "I'm taking a break from carrying your burdens. I'm really tired of the trouble you cause. Try again later." God is patient. His love means He's fully dependable. He said He'll carry your load, and He will.

We do a couple really foolish things. First we try to carry our own load, thinking we're strong enough. Second we try to manage the trouble on our own because we don't want to bother God. It's sort of like having a truck available to haul a load of bricks, but carrying them on your own because you don't want to turn the ignition switch. Trucks are intended to carry bricks. God intends to carry our burdens. The decision is easy. Give up the burdens.

Dear God, You want me to give up the stress that puts
me in a bad place. Help me say no when necessary
and allow You to carry the weight of all those things
I can't handle or control. Amen.

LOVE YOUR ENEMIES

"But I tell you, love your enemies and pray for those who persecute you, that you may be children of your Father in heaven."
MATTHEW 5:44–45 NIV

We all have people we don't like—and people we *really* don't like. You might even call them your enemies. Whether it's a long-time rival, a bully at school, or someone who always mistreats you, it's easy to return hate with hate.

It was accepted in Jesus' time, much like ours, to love friends and hate enemies. But Jesus takes what's accepted and puts a radical twist on it by saying we should not only love our friends, but also our enemies. And just as we pray for our friends, we should pray for our enemies. Not spiteful prayers demanding justice and vindication, but loving and kind prayers for the people who mistreat us.

If we hate our enemies, we're just like everyone else. And we're not supposed to be like everyone else! God wants us to be distinct from the world, pointing others to Jesus by what we believe, think, say, and do.

So what enemy can you pray for today?

Jesus, it's not easy returning kindness for hatred and prayers for pain. But You know that. You were treated horribly during Your ministry, and You loved and forgave. Help me to have Your spirit and strength to do the same. Amen.

YARDSTICK ARROGANCE

I give each of you this warning: Don't think you are better than you really are. Be honest in your evaluation of yourselves, measuring yourselves by the faith God has given us.
ROMANS 12:3 NLT

Did you know God talks about yardsticks? No? He warns us about measuring ourselves against others. Why? He knows that we'll have a tendency to think we come out looking either a lot better or a lot worse depending on who we have in mind.

That type of comparison leaves us feeling depressed or arrogant. We do a few things better than other people and suddenly feel that God's pretty lucky to have us on His team. We look for the faults of others, and we're quick to find them. Suddenly we're even better than we thought because we don't do the same sinful things they do. Our yardsticks get a workout.

God wants us to stop trying to measure another person's life. He wants us to banish arrogance and admit that if we measure ourselves by God's perfect standard, we fail. When we really see our own imperfection we should humbly put the yardsticks away.

Dear God, help me see that You measure my life by the yardstick of rescue that Jesus created when He paid for my sin on the cross. Remind me there's never room for arrogance from someone who's never been perfect. Amen.

THE TEST OF LOVE

"If you love me, you will obey my commands."
JOHN 14:15 NCV

A lot of people say they love God. But not everyone who says they love God obeys Him and does what He says. Can you love God and be disobedient? No.

Your obedience to God *proves* your love for Him. If you love God, you will listen to Him. If you don't love God, you will disobey Him and do whatever you want. You can't both love and rebel against God at the same time. This is why Jesus said, "Why do you call me, 'Lord, Lord,' and do not do what I say?" (Luke 6:46 NIV).

We naturally want to please those we love. It hurts us when we know we've hurt or disappointed someone we care about. So we strive to show our love in ways that please the other person. We may not *like* doing the dishes, but we know it really blesses Mom. We may dislike basketball, but we attend a game anyway because our friend enjoys it. Similarly, our obedience to God shows Him how much we love Him and want to please Him.

Actions win over words every time. How well are you loving God?

Lord, please forgive me for disobeying You at times.
I truly want to follow You and make You Lord of my life.
Help me live in obedience so my love for You shows
and my life is pleasing to You. Amen.

*Obviously, I'm not trying to win the approval of people,
but of God. If pleasing people were my goal,
I would not be Christ's servant.*
GALATIANS 1:10 NLT

Paul confronted the believers in Galatia for following a twisted version of the Gospel that wasn't the true message at all (see v. 6). Paul stated there is only one true message—the way of Jesus—but people were confusing His message, changing it, and causing people to turn away from the real truth (see v. 7). So Paul strongly called for punishment of those who changed God's message (see vv. 8–9).

Paul clearly stepped on some toes! He knew his words would offend some people, but he didn't care (see v. 10). He wasn't out to win people's approval—he only wanted to please God.

What truths in God's Word are hard for you to swallow? Do you find yourself trying to be "tolerant" and watering down God's message so it's more comfortable for you and others in our culture? Are you afraid to offend others by sharing God's truth?

Who are you trying to please? Others or Him?

God, help me boldly share the truth in love. Help me to be sensitive to others, but not back down from what I know is true from Your Word. I know it will offend people sometimes, but I don't want to please others. I just want to please You. Amen.

NOTHING TO BE EMBARRASSED ABOUT

*Always be prepared to give an answer to everyone
who asks you to give the reason for the hope that you have.
But do this with gentleness and respect.*
1 PETER 3:15 NIV

Peter was a disciple of Jesus. He was impulsive. He acted before he thought. It got him into trouble.

One of his "awkward" moments came a few hours before Jesus' death. Peter was in the crowd hoping to see Jesus. Three times he was asked if he was a follower of Jesus. He said no. The man who wrote, "Always be prepared to give an answer to everyone who asks you to give the reason for the hope that you have," didn't give a truthful answer that night.

Jesus forgave Peter. He told Peter that he would be used to start the church. The lessons Peter learned helped him understand the hope we have is worth sharing and there is no reason to be embarrassed. People want to know what makes us different. We should quit hiding the many gifts God has asked us to distribute. The greatest of these gifts is love.

*Dear God, You don't want me to respond like Peter, but I'm pretty
sure I have. When others ask if I know You, it's easy to say no.
I do follow You, and You're worth sharing. Others need to know
that You're always the top headline of the day. Amen.*

FAITH

*Faith means being sure of the things we hope for
and knowing that something is real
even if we do not see it.*
HEBREWS 11:1 NCV

"God, I don't get it! Why did this happen? I just don't understand!"

Ever had these thoughts? Everyone does. These thoughts can be accompanied with anger, grief, disappointment, or even a sense of rebellion—wanting to turn your back on God. But circumstances that prompt these thoughts are what test and prove your trust in God. *Faith* is to believe in God's goodness, love, and sovereign control. . .no matter what. It's being *certain* of God's good character, even when you may not see it. It's being *sure* that God loves you and is taking care of you, even when He feels distant and silent and like He's not even there. Faith says, "Even when I don't understand, I will choose You, God. I will trust You, no matter what."

Does God have your full faith? Can you trust Him, whatever happens?

-

Sovereign God, I want to believe in You. I want to trust that You do have good plans and something positive can come out of all this bad. So I put my faith in You, and I choose to believe in Your goodness and love. Despite my circumstances, I choose to trust You. Amen.

*Then I saw "a new heaven and a new earth," for the first
heaven and the first earth had passed away. . . . And I heard
a loud voice from the throne saying, "Look! God's dwelling place
is now among the people, and he will dwell with them. . . .
He will wipe every tear from their eyes. There will be no more
death or mourning or crying or pain, for the old order
of things has passed away."*
REVELATION 21:1–4 NIV

At the core of the Christian faith is the belief that we'll spend
eternity with God if we confess our sins and put our faith in Him.
But how often do we really think about the hope of heaven? Or
imagine it? Or study what the Bible says about it? Most of the
time heaven is this vague hope that we'll join God "somewhere
up there" when we die.

But eternity with God is an exciting thing! Revelation 21
says God will live among us—we'll actually *see* Him (see v. 3)!
There will be no sun or moon because God's glory will be bright
enough to provide all light (see v. 23). God's light will eternally
shine, and there will never be night (see v. 25). There will be
no pain, no death, no shame or deceit (see vv. 4, 27), only
happiness, joy, and perfection.

Imagine!

*Lord, the hope of heaven overwhelms me.
Thank You for saving me! I can't wait to live with You. Amen.*

LOOK UP

Think about what is up there, not about what is here on earth.
COLOSSIANS 3:2 CEV

I love getting outside and taking walks or hiking trails. But too often my gaze stays on my feet and the path immediately before me. I consciously have to pull my eyes up and remind myself to take in the beauty of my surroundings as I walk.

Life is like that, too. It's so easy to keep our eyes focused on the immediate—schoolwork, athletic performance, feeling accepted, frustration with parents, etc. It's hard to look past tomorrow, let alone beyond high school! But God wants you to pull your eyes all the way up—to Him. He wants you to look beyond your present circumstances and remember what's truly important—eternal life with Him.

So release your worries, realign your priorities, and let go of the temporary things here on earth. Keep your eyes and your mind focused on what truly lasts. Look up and see the beauty of God all around you instead of staying focused on the dull path before you.

Thank You, Father, for the hope of heaven. For the promise that someday everything will be perfect and all the stress and worry and pain I experience on earth will be gone. Help me to lift my eyes and thoughts to You and be filled with joy, peace, and hope. Amen.

*Don't hit back; discover beauty in everyone. If you've got
it in you, get along with everybody. Don't insist on getting even;
that's not for you to do. "I'll do the judging,"
says God. "I'll take care of it."*
ROMANS 12:17–19 MSG

Maybe you've heard of the Hatfields and McCoys. These two
families lived in Virginia and Kentucky in 1863. They started
a feud and never seemed to get over it. They fought and killed
each other, and the feud continued for generations.

We can act like these two families. Someone hurts us and
we strike back. Soon no one remembers peace.

God wants us to get along with others to the best of our
ability. He doesn't want us to get even, but to forgive. He doesn't
want us to act as judge, but to love. The best news is God
promises to take care of the issue.

Others won't be perfect, but God wants us to find something
good in them.

When you try to get even there will be no winners. When
you offer love, something wonderful happens. God influences
two hearts—one of which is yours.

*Dear God, it's hard to understand why You'd want me to allow
myself to be wronged, yet this is Your wisdom on the subject.
You compensate for any struggle I face by offering love,
acceptance, and strength for the challenge of injustice.
You're much better at judging than I'll ever be. Amen.*

FACING PERSECUTION

"If we are thrown into the blazing furnace, the God we serve is able to deliver us from it, and he will deliver us from Your Majesty's hand. But even if he does not, we want you to know, Your Majesty, that we will not serve your gods or worship the image of gold you have set up."
DANIEL 3:17–18 NIV

Sometimes being a Christian has consequences. People might make fun of you, bully you, or label you as *weird*. Sometimes you won't be able to do what your friends are doing. And in many cases, especially in other countries, being a Christian can mean facing physical harm.

God can save us and protect us from those consequences. But what if He doesn't? Shadrach, Meshach, and Abednego understood that God was powerful enough to save them from any persecution they might face. But they also understood that God doesn't always "deliver" us in the way we expect and allows us to face consequences and experience pain.

Is your faith as strong as Shadrach's, Meshach's, and Abednego's? Are you resolved to obey God, even if He doesn't keep the pain away? Are you committed to follow Him—no matter what?

Jesus, help me not to give in when I feel pressure to go against You. Help me stand strong in my faith and have the courage to face whatever happens. Amen.

MIXED EMOTIONS

Yet I am always with you; you hold me by my right hand.
You guide me with your counsel, and afterward
you will take me into glory.
PSALM 73:23–24 NIV

Sometimes life just doesn't seem fair. Right? Nonbelievers seem to have better lives and fewer worries. The jerks get favored while the good guys are overlooked. Cheaters get ahead while those who play by the rules suffer. So. Not. Fair.

Asaph, the writer of Psalm 73, struggled with the same complaint. He envied nonbelievers because their life seemed blessed (see vv. 2–14). The unfairness greatly distressed him until he realized their final destiny (see v. 17). They lived on slippery ground (see v. 18), and their eventual judgment would be swift and hard (see vv. 19–20). Asaph realized that though life may not play out fairly, it's far better to be close to God (see v. 28).

Being a Christian doesn't mean life will be easier or perfectly just. We'll suffer. Things won't be fair. Sometimes the bad guys will win. . .for now. But we have God on our side and His presence in our life. He'll make everything right in the end.

God, injustice makes me so mad. I hate when the bad guys
win. But I am comforted that You are always with Your
people. You never leave us, and we have eternal life
with You. Thank You that fairness will win in the end. Amen.

SELF BETRAYAL

"Where your treasure is, there your heart will be also."
MATTHEW 6:21 NIV

Your heart is the most honest, yet devious thing about you. It understands what's important to you even when your mind is in denial. Try to keep things hidden and your heart will betray you. If you think a girl is pretty, your heart sends a message to your face. The result can be embarrassing.

Give your heart godly wisdom and it'll encourage godly living. Invest time in what God told us to avoid and the heart can become desperately wicked. Your actions will always prove a change in priority.

When your mind doesn't spend time with God your heart evaluates and recalculates what's really important to you and makes this new preference its greatest treasure. You may not want this change. You may not want to have a different focus than God. You can even deny the existence of change, but the heart is honest enough to evaluate your real priorities and prove what's on your mind.

Argue with the heart all you want, but for the heart to keep God in first place your mind has to keep God in first place.

Dear God, guard my heart. Help me do more than say
the right words. Bring my mind and heart together
so when others are around me long enough,
they can see You really are the most important part
of my life. I need You to be my greatest treasure. Amen.

WHO'S YOUR UMPIRE?

*Let the peace that Christ gives control your thinking,
because you were all called together in one
body to have peace. Always be thankful.*
COLOSSIANS 3:15 NCV

When you have a decision to make, everyone always says to "pray about it." But what does that mean? Okay, so I ask God about what He wants me to do. . .then what?

Then you wait for peace.

God's Word says to let peace be our umpire. When an opportunity or decision is pitched your way, God stands behind you as the umpire. He'll tell you whether or not to swing for the ball by the peace you feel. What decision makes you feel 100 percent at peace—no doubts, no nagging questions, no second-guessing? Just a calm sense of rightness. That's how you know what God wants you to do.

Any decision that doesn't bring peace means it's out! God wants you to turn it down or pass it by because something better is coming your way or maybe now isn't the right time.

What decisions are you facing today? What is your sense of peace telling you to do?

*God, thank You for letting peace be my umpire,
guiding me about what to do. Help me to strongly sense
your peace as I make decisions. Amen.*

*"Simply put, if you're not willing to take what is dearest
to you, whether plans or people, and kiss it good-bye,
you can't be my disciple."*
LUKE 14:33 MSG

Following God isn't just about following rules, going to church,
and reading your Bible. It's not about being good and waiting
for God's approval in return. Or making your own plans and
asking for His blessing on what *you* decide. Following God
means total surrender.

Jesus demands *everything* from you—your rights, your
dreams, your plans for the future, your life.

Now, wait a second! That's so harsh! The cost *is* high, but
the reward is even greater. Following Jesus wasn't meant to be
easy. It demands sacrifice, and it shows what you truly love. If
you love someone or something more than you love God, you
won't be willing to give it up. And God wants to be first in your
life, your greatest love.

Are you willing to follow Him? What do you need to
surrender?

*Whew, Jesus. You ask a lot from me. But I also know that
You gave up everything for me—leaving Your home in heaven,
restricting Yourself in a human body, and dying a horrible death
to pay for my sins. I want to love You that much, too.
But it's scary. Lord, I surrender to You. Amen.*

LEAP OF FAITH

*Then Peter got down out of the boat, walked on the water
and came toward Jesus. But when he saw the wind,
he was afraid and, beginning to sink, cried out, "Lord, save me!"
Immediately Jesus reached out his hand and caught him.
"You of little faith," he said, "why did you doubt?"*
MATTHEW 14:29–31 NIV

It's one thing to *say* we trust God. But when we actually have
to do it—it can be pretty scary! To step out of a boat onto solid
ground, no problem! To step out of a boat into the middle of a
lake to *walk* on water during a windy night with no life vest? Um,
seriously?

Even for Peter, that was a scary leap! But the moment Peter
cried out, Jesus was right there, catching him, keeping him tight
in His grip. Yes, trusting God can be scary. But He's always right
there to catch us, never leaving us, never letting go.

Taking a leap of faith means stepping out of the familiar into
something that may seem crazy, but it also means experiencing
the joy and warmth of the Father's arms when He catches you. It
means feeling the intensity of His grip on you. And suddenly, His
voice, His touch, and His presence become tangible in your life.

*God, trusting You can be difficult. Help me to trust You
and experience You like Peter did. Help me to feel
Your grip on my life. Amen.*

A TIME TO DECIDE

We don't have a priest who is out of touch with our reality.
He's been through weakness and testing, experienced it all—
all but the sin. So let's walk right up to him and get what he
is so ready to give. Take the mercy, accept the help.
HEBREWS 4:15–16 MSG

Some decisions are simple, like what cereal to eat for breakfast. Some are hard, like what college to attend. Decisions are complicated by how they affect others and whether they reflect godly character.

The Bible says we have access to God's wisdom and guidance whenever we need it. The Holy Spirit helps influence decision-making, but Jesus is also available to represent our struggles to God.

Jesus is perfect for the role because He was once like us. He lived on earth and was tempted and tested, but Jesus never sinned. So when we ask for help, He understands why we need it.

Whenever we have questions, whenever we need mercy, whenever we just want to be with Him—we must be bold. Ask. He listens.

Dear God, You don't want me to keep my struggles hidden.
I can share them with You. I can expect Your guidance.
I can hold on to Your mercy and forgiveness. There are tough
decisions I will make. Help me always check
in with You first. Amen.

*This is the confidence we have in approaching God:
that if we ask anything according to his will, he hears us.
And if we know that he hears us—whatever we ask—
we know that we have what we asked of him.*
1 JOHN 5:14–15 NIV

All good things come to those who wait. Right? But sometimes we wait and wait and nothing happens. We pray, and God doesn't answer.

Many times there's growth that needs to take place in our life before we're ready for God's reply. Sometimes we hear from God only after we've persisted in asking (see Luke 18:1–8). Persistently praying also reveals our faithfulness and teaches us to keep praying without giving up (see Galatians 6:9).

Sometimes God's answer is simply *no*. Are you still able to trust God and believe He is good when He doesn't allow you to have what you want? Is He enough? Or are you clinging too hard to something else?

God could be denying your prayers because you're asking with wrong motives (see James 4:3). If your request comes from selfishness to satisfy yourself and not to glorify God, chances are God isn't going to grant it.

When you pray, know that God has a plan. He is good, and He will not withhold any good thing from you!

*Lord, teach me to pray according to Your will,
with pure motives, and with patient persistence. Amen.*

A VERY BAD DAY

"I came naked from my mother's womb, and I will be naked when I leave. The Lord gave me what I had, and the Lord has taken it away. Praise the name of the Lord!"
JOB 1:21 NLT

Job was a very rich man. But he lost *everything*—all his livestock, farmhands, servants, and children—in *one day* (see Job 1:13–18)! In a flash, he went from wealthy to bankrupt, from proud papa to childless man. Just. Like. That. But he didn't respond with anger and shouting. Undone, he fell to the ground *in worship* (see v. 20)! With tears streaming down his face, he praised the Lord.

When we suffer, it's natural to question God—to ask why and seek understanding. As Job continued to suffer, he sure asked tough questions and demanded some answers from God. But God never explained Himself—He just said, "I'm big. I'm good. I'm in control. Will you trust Me?"

Do you trust God that much? When bad things happen or life takes a crazy curve, do you get angry or praise God amid the confusion and pain? Do you demand answers or simply trust God, even if you don't understand? Do you wrestle—or do you surrender?

God, sometimes it's hard to praise You, even when it hurts. To believe in Your goodness, even when nothing seems good. Help me to trust You and praise You like Job. Amen.

*Be kind and compassionate to one another,
forgiving each other, just as in Christ God forgave you.*
EPHESIANS 4:32 NIV

Today's technology makes gossip a whole lot easier. It's so simple and easy to say things online about someone that you would never say face-to-face. Facebook, e-mail, blogs, texting, and IMs make it easy to engage in word wars that are less than encouraging and kind. And far more hurtful.

Watch what you say—especially in print. Don't engage in mean-spirited talk about others. If things are being said about you, don't respond angrily. Give yourself time to calm down and think of a gentle response. And always work to take the conversation offline and speak face-to-face or on the phone.

If verbal bullying continues in person or online, tell a trusted adult what's happening. If you know of someone being harassed, don't be a bystander! Gently shut down the conversation or stick up for the person. And if mean comments are flying around about you, work to forgive the person and respond with love and grace.

Lord, please forgive me for saying mean things about others, especially online. Help me to forgive those who say mean things about me and to respond the way You want me to, not in hurt or anger. Amen.

PRAISE THE LORD!

Praise the LORD! Give thanks to the LORD, for he is good!
His faithful love endures forever.
PSALM 106:1 NLT

The Bible commands us to *praise* the Lord and *give thanks* to Him because His faithful love endures forever. Why should God's people be commanded to do something that should come naturally?

How many people have you told about that amazing movie you saw? The gripping book you read? The fun song you heard? Did you speak highly of it and express enthusiastic approval toward it? If so, you praised the thing you enjoyed.

If you're not praising God, examine why. Have you stopped enjoying God? Why? It's easy to lose sight of who God is and what He's done. God can become like an old Christmas gift— we experience joy and excitement upon first receiving Him, but after a while He gets shoved in a closet and forgotten about. But God's love is faithful and will always be there for you, even when your love for Him fades. The love of God never expires—He loves you now and for eternity. No matter what.

Thank You, God!

Lord, I praise You today for Your incredible love. I can be mean to You, hurt You, and deliberately disobey You, but You still forgive me and cover me with Your love and grace. Your love is powerful, God, and worthy of my praise! Amen.

MISTAKES WERE MADE

The godly may trip seven times, but they will get up again.
But one disaster is enough to overthrow the wicked.
PROVERBS 24:16 NLT

Being a Christian doesn't mean you no longer make mistakes. It doesn't mean that you'll never sin again. It doesn't even mean that you aren't tempted anymore. The truth is you might feel like you let God down more after you accept His redemption gift than before.

Did you know this is the way our spiritual enemy wants us to think? Satan wants us to believe that when we become Christians we'll never let God down. He's downright giddy thinking up ways for us to feel guilty for bad behavior.

It's true that God wants us to obey His commands, but He doesn't want us to feel condemned. Why? Because when we feel condemned we give up. When we give up we no longer try. When we no longer try we accept the enemy's lie as truth.

Get back up and start walking again. Jesus paid for all sin. This includes the one that knocked you down. The Christian man will trip—and he'll get back up.

Dear God, keep my mind and heart from believing that when I sin You no longer love me. I want to serve You well, so when I fail help me admit my mistakes, accept Your forgiveness, and get back to work. Help me ignore the words that tempt me to accept defeat. Amen.

WHAT'S YOUR STATUS?

Everything they do is just to show off in front of others. . . .
They love the best seats at banquets and the front seats in
the meeting places. And when they are in the market,
they like to have people greet them as their teachers.
MATTHEW 23:5–7 CEV

The Pharisees were all about status. They flaunted their position as religious leaders, strutting around in pride and arrogance. And Jesus condemned them for it.

It's easy to point our fingers at the Pharisees and say how bad they were. But we are status-seekers, too. Are you tempted to hide your friendship with someone when the more popular kids come around? Do you always try to sit where you know you'll be noticed? Do you drive yourself in academics or athletics because you seek the attention that comes with it? Do you wear name-brand clothes because you want the status of being cool and stylish?

Jesus says, "If you put yourself above others, you will be put down. But if you humble yourself, you will be honored" (Matthew 23:12 CEV). Status among our peers isn't what's truly important. Make it a point to serve instead of show off.

God, please forgive me for thinking I'm better than others and
for seeking the status and approval of my friends instead of You.
Help me to take a backseat and serve others, like You,
by focusing on others and not myself. Amen.

ROADBLOCKS AHEAD!

"I've had it with you! You're hopeless, you religion scholars, you Pharisees! Frauds! Your lives are roadblocks to God's kingdom."
MATTHEW 23:13 MSG

"Christians are just a bunch of hypocrites!"

We've all heard someone say it. Hypocrisy is one of the biggest reasons nonbelievers want nothing to do with Christianity. Pastors are caught stealing church funds. Christian girls get pregnant. Christian guys are pulled over and slapped with a DUI. Sin has pretty big consequences.

As a Christian, you represent Jesus to everyone around you. You aren't perfect, and you won't represent Him perfectly all the time. But you need to remove the roadblocks to God's kingdom by matching your actions with your words. Do people see you going to church on Sunday, but cussing and cutting down others during the week? Do they see you pray before your meals, but be disrespectful to your parents and teachers? Do they know you're a Christian, but are turned off by your arrogance and pride?

The world is watching, whether you're aware or not. Are your words and actions inviting people into heaven—or turning them away?

Lord, I know I mess up and seem like a hypocrite. I'm glad people can look to You as the perfect example instead of me. But I don't want to turn people away from You because of the sin in my life. Show me how I need to change so others are drawn to You through me. Amen.

CLEAN HEART

"You Pharisees are so careful to clean the outside of the cup and the dish, but inside you are filthy—full of greed and wickedness! Fools! Didn't God make the inside as well as the outside? So clean the inside by giving gifts to the poor, and you will be clean all over."
LUKE 11:39–41 NLT

Jesus was ticked off at the Pharisees because they had impure motives. They did all the right things—but for all the wrong reasons. They were so careful to follow the rules and be "good," but their hearts were self-righteous and full of pride. Jesus saw through their sham and said when their motives were pure, then their "good works" would be acceptable.

Jesus isn't concerned about our behavior—He's concerned about our hearts. Because when your heart is right, then proper behavior will naturally follow. Why do you attend church? Because your parents make you, or because you want to? Why do you read your Bible? Because you want to or because you feel guilty if you don't?

Jesus isn't concerned about you following a set of rules—doing what you're *supposed* to do. He wants you to follow Him willingly, because you *want* to. Ask yourself: Why do I do what I do? Whom am I doing it for?

Jesus, forgive me for doing things because they'll make me look good on the outside, when I have the wrong motive on the inside. Clean me from the inside out. Amen.

THE CONTROL STRATEGY

Run away from infantile indulgence. Run after mature righteousness—faith, love, peace—joining those who are in honest and serious prayer before God. Refuse to get involved in inane discussions; they always end up in fights.
2 TIMOTHY 2:22–23 MSG

Consoles, controllers, cartridges, downloadable content, online play, and *USB drive* are all video gaming terms. These games are a little like board games, and yet almost nothing like them. They invite competition, strategy, team building, and a sense of accomplishment.

Gaming is a culture all its own. There are conventions, magazines, forums, and online chat. Each is dedicated to growing the influence of gaming. The strategy is working.

The big decision for a Christian guy is how much gaming is too much. You might have to wrestle with which games might be appropriate and evaluate where gaming fits in your list of priorities.

When you don't grapple with these issues it becomes very easy to let gaming control every available moment. It's also easier for gaming culture to unseat God from His role as life leader. Chase God's character, hang on to His words, and hang out with those who see greater value in God's kingdom than in a virtual one.

Dear God, if You really are in control of my life then let me serve You in a way that proves You're more important to me than anything—including gaming. Help my walk, talk, and heart to speak nothing less than the language of Your love. Amen.

PRAYING FOR THE NATION

Everyone must submit to governing authorities.
For all authority comes from God and those in positions
of authority have been placed there by God.
ROMANS 13:1 NLT

Politics. . .*blech*! Who cares what's going on in the government? It's hard to understand what the news anchors are talking about, and it's *bo*-ring anyway. God's got it all covered, right?

While the Bible is full of stories of God moving people and nations into power and out of power, that doesn't mean we stick our head in the sand and ignore what's happening politically. We have an amazing blessing in America to vote and shape our government. Our active participation or passive disinterest will directly affect our future.

You will be a voting citizen someday. It's important that you pay attention in history class, discuss with your teachers and parents the problems and decisions our nation faces, and learn to think critically about the decisions political leaders make.

Most importantly, we need to pray for our leaders— locally, statewide, and nationally. Pray for God to place the correct people in office, for corruption to be exposed, and for cooperation among political parties so they can work together for the common good.

Lord, I pray for our government. The problems are many,
but I pray that You would lead and guide our leaders
to make the best decisions for our country. Amen.

WHO'S THE BOMB?

*Don't think you are better than you really are. Be honest
in your evaluation of yourselves, measuring yourselves
by the faith God has given us.*
ROMANS 12:3 NLT

It's *so* tempting to bask in others' praise, isn't it? To glory in your
athletic ability and strut down the halls at school. To pat yourself
on the back for your academic achievements. To take credit for
your musical ability or physical appearance. To pride yourself in
the fact that at least you aren't like *them*.

But the credit doesn't belong to you. God made you and
gave you the talents you have. We owe everything to Him. And
without His grace, we wouldn't be anybody. So put arrogance
aside and thank God for blessing you. When others praise you,
use the opportunity to point them to Jesus, the giver of all good
gifts. Use your talents for God's glory, not your own.

*Please forgive me, Jesus. You never lorded yourself over anyone,
and You were always quick to give praise to the Father. Help me
to use my talents for Your kingdom, to use them as a witness to
others and not for my own personal gain or fame. Amen.*

INTEGRITY

"Everything that is hidden will be found out, and every secret will be known. Whatever you say in the dark will be heard when it is day. Whatever you whisper in a closed room will be shouted from the housetops."
LUKE 12:2–3 CEV

Have you ever breathed a sigh of relief when your sibling took the blame for something you did? Feel lucky that you didn't get caught cheating on your history quiz? Ever watch something you knew you shouldn't? You may think you got away with it, but God sees everything. One day everything will be revealed, and everyone will be judged.

Don't be caught like the Pharisees! Jesus revealed them to the world for who they really were. The Pharisees weren't upstanding religious leaders to be imitated and followed; they were greedy, self-righteous, wicked men whom Jesus publicly judged and condemned.

Keeping up a good image and hiding their sin—that was the Pharisees' main goal. Scrap what others think, and make pleasing Jesus your main goal. It doesn't matter if you will or won't get away with something here on earth. You won't get away with it with God.

God, help me to come clean about my sin and not hide it or let others take the blame for it. Help me be more concerned about pleasing You than maintaining a good image. Amen.

TRUTH DEFENDERS

Stay alert! Watch out for your great enemy, the devil.
He prowls around like a roaring lion,
looking for someone to devour.
1 PETER 5:8 NLT

Have you ever wondered why God would ask us to be loving, kind, and patient and then ask us to be warriors? What exactly does a God-warrior look like anyway?

God-warriors struggle against those who deny the truth of God's Word. We use the armor of God to hold ground against Satan (see Ephesians 6:10–18). We stand watch for faith attacks that could weaken our commitment to God. We're warriors relying on God's strength.

Perhaps the greatest reason we're asked to be warrior-ready is to recognize the truth of God's Word and the lies of our spiritual enemy. If we refuse to stand firm then we'll be crushed when we're weak.

God built guys to be protectors, and He doesn't want us to stop short of being guardians of His truth, which can be found in every page of the Bible. These same words are used for correcting error, instructing others, and providing the training needed for right living (see 2 Timothy 3:16).

Dear God, You want me to be strong. The hope that's in me
relies on the truth of Your Word. Through the words I read
I understand Your ways, and I learn how foolish it is
to believe Your words don't matter. Give me the strength
I need to stand for Your truth. Amen.

HOLINESS VS. HAPPINESS

"Make yourselves holy for I am holy. . . . I am God who brought you up out of the land of Egypt. Be holy because I am holy."
LEVITICUS 11:44–45 MSG

God wants us to be happy, right? Well, yes. But God is far more concerned with our holiness than our happiness. Numerous times throughout the Bible, God commands His people to be holy. Not once does He command us to be happy.

While God does desire to bless us, He has a far greater purpose for us than happiness. When we choose to follow God, we leave our old habits behind and become a new person. We strive to become holy as God is holy—reflecting His goodness and character to all those around us. Be careful not to make decisions based on how happy it will make you. "It's okay to do this, have this, or be with this person because God wants me to be happy" is dangerous logic. Instead ask yourself, "Is doing this, having this, or being with this person going to draw me closer to God and help me grow spiritually?"

Paul told Timothy, "For God saved us and called us to live a holy life" (2 Timothy 1:9 NLT). Are you pursuing happiness more than holiness?

God, help me to care more about holiness than happiness. Give me strength to sacrifice happiness when holiness requires it and trust that You will bring joy and blessing from my obedience. Amen.

GOD IS WATCHING

The eyes of the LORD are everywhere,
keeping watch on the wicked and the good.
PROVERBS 15:3 NIV

My parents had rules. And one of those rules restricted me from watching any movie above a PG rating without their permission. There were countless times I'd spend the night at a friend's house, and he'd pop in a PG-13 movie.

It's just PG-13, I'd think to myself. *My parents won't need to know. I don't need to say anything.*

But God's conviction and my conscience would never let me get away with it. I knew God was watching, even if my parents weren't. And God wanted me to obey my parents. So I'd call and ask for permission before any movies started—every time.

A lot of times I felt like an idiot in front of my friends, especially if my parents didn't want me to watch the movie and I had to suggest something else. But the momentary embarrassment was worth the rewards. I didn't have to battle a guilty conscience. I built trust with my parents, which eventually gave me greater freedom from the rules. And most of all, I know I pleased God with my obedience to Him and my parents.

What areas of compromise tempt you the most?

God, help me to listen when You convict me and do the right thing, even if it means I'll look foolish or feel embarrassed. You are always watching, and I want to please You. Amen.

DANGER IN THE REPLAY

You will keep in perfect peace all who trust in you,
all whose thoughts are fixed on you!
ISAIAH 26:3 NLT

You have a very creative mind. Artists imagine a setting and then paint. Musicians imagine music and soon others listen.

Our minds can imagine what it would be like to hurt someone who's been mean. We can have sinful thoughts about a girl. We can spend time imagining things that aren't currently on God's agenda for our lives.

When we allow our minds to play imaginary films that feature us carrying out sinful actions we really need to step back and urgently ask God for help.

We can dismiss our own objections by saying, "I'd never actually do this," but by allowing mental sin films to play—and replay—we can come to the point where what we've seen in our mind becomes action.

In those moments we no longer recognize God's peace, but refuse to give God a second thought. Why? When we're committing sin we act as if God shouldn't have a say in how we live.

Dear God, keep my eyes, heart, and mind fixed on You.
May my thought life conform to Your desire for purity.
Help me learn to stop impure thoughts and send them away.
I can only do this when I intentionally come back to You. Amen.

BUCKLE DOWN

All athletes are disciplined in their training. They do it to win a prize that will fade away, but we do it for an eternal prize.
1 CORINTHIANS 9:25 NLT

Sometimes it's hard to worship, because you just don't feel like it. You don't want to be at church. You don't want to pray. You don't want to read your Bible. You just want to leave God alone for a while and do what you want.

A relationship with God is just like any other commitment—it takes work. You may not feel like going to swim practice every day or doing your homework after school, but you do it anyway. Sure, maybe you're only doing it because you have to. But you're also doing it because on a deeper level, you want to—you want to improve your swim times and keep your grades up.

God is no different. We may not always *feel* like worshipping Him or spending time with Him, but we need to discipline ourselves to do it anyway. Only when we're disciplined and stay committed—not just showing up to practice here and there, but *every* day—will we see growth.

God, help me to discipline myself to work at my relationship with You. A lot of times I don't feel like it, but I know putting in the time and effort will help me grow spiritually— and that's a lasting prize worth pursuing. Amen.

ENTITLED

You must have the same attitude that Christ Jesus had. . . .
When he appeared in human form, he humbled himself
in obedience to God and died a criminal's death on a cross.
PHILIPPIANS 2:5, 7–8 NLT

Entitlement has become an epidemic in our country. The belief that you have the right to have, do, or get something, or that you *deserve* to be given something, is a disease that cripples you and those around you.

Jesus never felt entitled. He was almighty, infinitely powerful, and deserving of honor and glory, but He gave up His divine rights and privileges and didn't cling to them. He willingly lowered Himself and limited Himself as a human being, even dying the most shameful death possible.

What rights and privileges are you clinging to? What do you complain about giving up?

Jesus, please help me to have an attitude like You.
You willingly humbled Yourself and let go. When life doesn't
seem fair or demands a sacrifice, help me do the same. Amen.

FORGIVENESS AFTER FAILURE

Godly sorrow brings repentance that leads to salvation and leaves no regret, but worldly sorrow brings death.
2 CORINTHIANS 7:10 NIV

God isn't too worried when we're sad because He never promised unending happiness. Sorrow has a purpose, but we don't always know what we're supposed to do with it.

Sadness at the loss of someone we love allows us to express sympathy when others have a similar experience. Sadness at the loss of a dream leads us to reevaluate priorities. Sadness at the loss of purity, truthfulness, and integrity can lead us to turn away from what we've done allowing God to restore us. This last loss is filled with second chances, but it all depends on how we deal with the sorrow that arrives after the choice to sin.

Those who don't know Jesus can also have sorrow, but what they feel may be because they got caught or they can't find hope and forgiveness. Sorrow can leave them wondering how they'll ever get over it.

Sorrow that turns us back to God helps us understand there is a future after failure.

Dear God, thank You for the reminder that when I'm frustrated with myself, You're waiting for my return. You offer second chances, but that means I need to move away from the things that led me to this place of sorrow. Thanks for letting me return every time I fail. Amen.

BE CONTENT

They are like hungry dogs that are never satisfied.
They are like shepherds who don't know what they are doing.
They all have gone their own way; all they want to
do is satisfy themselves.
ISAIAH 56:11 NCV

By human nature, we want to satisfy ourselves. We want the latest technology, the newest phones, the trendy clothes. We want the best cable TV, the fastest Internet, the nicest cars. We want. . . we want. . .we want.

Even if we get what we want, it only satisfies for a while and then we want something else. It's a cycle that doesn't end—a trap we must consciously avoid.

Instead of complaining about what you *don't* have, stop and be grateful for what you *do* have. When your friend shows off her new iPhone, instead of being jealous, be grateful you have a cell phone, even if it's "just a flip phone." When your parents steer you toward the sale racks or thrift stores instead of brand-new, full-price clothes, be thankful they're even able to provide you with new clothing.

The secret of contentment is being grateful for what you have instead of searching for something to satisfy you. How content are you?

Lord, my human nature sees something new and shiny,
and I can't help but want it. Change my attitude.
Help me be content and grateful for what I do have. Amen.

PARENTAL UNITS

Children, obey your parents in the Lord, for this is right.
EPHESIANS 6:1 NIV

Parents may be annoying at times, but they do *a lot* for you. They work hard to provide money for you to buy new clothes, join athletic teams, have a cell phone and computer, and have food to eat. They run you around to all your practices and activities. They pay for you to attend summer camp or go on a family vacation.

Parents aren't perfect and everyone has faults, but spend time today honoring your parents. Make a list of everything they do and provide for you. How can you make their burden easier? How can you help out around the house? Maybe you can start doing your own laundry instead of expecting your mom to do it, or you can put the money you've earned toward summer camp fees instead of blowing it at Starbucks or the movies. Why not make dinner tonight for the family?

Whatever you decide to do, be sure to thank your parents today for all they do for you.

God, I can't imagine life without my parents. I may not always like them, but they take care of me the best they can. If I had to survive on my own, I'd be in a really tough place. So thank You for my mom and dad, and show me how I can honor and thank them today. Amen.

LIVING IN GRACE

You were saved by faith in God, who treats us much better than we deserve. This is God's gift to you, and not anything you have done on your own. It isn't something you have earned, so there is nothing you can brag about.
EPHESIANS 2:8–9 CEV

God's love isn't something we have to earn. He gives it freely. But too often we fall into the trap of living a performance-based faith. If you don't attend youth group every week, you're not a good Christian. If you don't read your Bible or spend time with God every day, God isn't pleased with you. If you keep committing the same sin, no matter how hard you try, God looks at you with disappointment.

Lies. All of them.

God gives you grace. He doesn't want you to live up to some standard of performance, feeling like you need to do certain things to earn His acceptance. He loves you right now, as you are, no matter what.

So give yourself grace. Toss the guilt you've been living under and experience the true freedom the Lord gives. You're His son, and He loves you whether you have it all together or you're a total mess.

And that's the truth.

Thank You, God, that I don't need to live in guilt. I don't have to feel like I need to measure up to some standard to earn Your acceptance. Help me to live in that grace and freedom today. Amen.

THE RUNAWAY RUNS BACK

"My son is here—given up for dead and now alive!
Given up for lost and now found!" And they began
to have a wonderful time.
LUKE 15:24 MSG

If you've never read the story of the Prodigal Son, spend some time in Luke 15 and get caught up. If you don't have time here's a crash course: The younger of two sons wanted an early inheritance. His dad gave him cash knowing he wouldn't make wise decisions. Dad was right. The son spent all his money, lost all personal pride, and ultimately saw pig food as fine dining. Once he realized his mistake he humbled himself and returned home knowing he'd blown it, but hoped he could get a job working for his dad. He was pretty nervous.

His dad came running from the house because he'd hoped his son would return. The idea of being a servant ended before it could be considered. His dad immediately put things together for a "welcome home" party celebrating the safe return of the runaway son.

When you've really made a mess of things don't wait—run back to God.

Dear God, when I'm a prodigal son I, too, will think that following Your instructions is hard, and I'll want to do things my way. It may not be pig food that turns me around, but when I turn, help me remember what You've done for me. I know You'll be waiting at the end of my run. Amen.

GROWTH HURTS

*We gladly suffer, because we know that suffering helps
us to endure. And endurance builds character, which gives
us a hope that will never disappoint us.*
ROMANS 5:3–5 CEV

No one *likes* to suffer, but suffering is necessary for growth.
First, it teaches endurance. When there's no way out of a
situation, you just have to slog through until it ends. And during
the slogging, your character develops. You either whine and cry
your way through it, or you learn to depend on God and bear it.
In the midst of enduring, you learn to take your eyes off yourself
and put them on Jesus. You learn patience and how to wait. You
learn faith.

And faith breeds hope. When we experience God's
presence, comfort, and faithfulness during hard times, we deepen
our trust and hope in Him. We come to know with certainty that
God is good. We *know* without a doubt He is in control and
has a plan. We *know* God is faithful and loves us. And with this
strong sense of faith, we can face any trial with hope—God is
there, and He will see us through, all the way to eternity.

How well do you face suffering? What lessons has God
taught you? What do you still need to learn?

*Thank You, Jesus, for all my sufferings. I may not like them,
but they do teach me a lot. Help me to face suffering
well and grow in my faith. Amen.*

BO-RING!

"See, I have chosen Bezalel son of Uri. . .and I have filled him with the Spirit of God. . .and with all kinds of skills—to make artistic designs for work in gold, silver and bronze, to cut and set stones, to work in wood, and to engage in all kinds of crafts."
EXODUS 31:2–5 NIV

You and your best bud—you like to do lots of things together, right? I mean, you'd get pretty bored if all you ever did was watch movies. There's no way you'd do the same ol' thing, at the same ol' time, *every* time you hung out. You'd both get tired of it.

God is a person, who desires to be in communication with you. And I'm pretty sure He gets bored when you spend time with Him doing the same ol' thing (reading your devotions and praying), at the same ol' time (in the morning or before bed), *every* time you hang out.

God creatively made you with special gifts and talents. What do you *love* to do? Play a musical instrument? Draw or paint? Write? Why not do that with God? Let your music, drawing, story, or art express your worship.

How can you have some fun hanging out with God today?

Wow, God, I never realized if I get bored spending time with You that You're probably bored, too! What new things do You want to do together? How can I get to know You in a new and fun way?

CONVERSATIONS

The LORD would speak to Moses face to face,
as one speaks to a friend.
EXODUS 33:11 NIV

So we know we can talk to God, just like we talk to our friends. It doesn't have to be all formal and stiff, like we're addressing an honorable judge. We can just express ourselves to Him however we want.

But here's the kicker. . .*God talks back!*

Yep, you heard right. God talks back to you, just like a friend. Prayer is a two-way conversation. But how much chattering do *you* do? Can God get a word in edgewise? Do you even wait for Him to speak? Or do you just say your piece and then rush off?

It's pretty annoying when a friend talks your ear off. Lucky for us, God never tunes us out, but He also has some things to say. Do you take the time to listen? Some call this *listening prayer*—taking the time to be quiet, silent, and open to what God wants to say to us. God can communicate in an audible voice, but usually He speaks in a small, still way within our hearts.

When you're still and silent, what thoughts, images, or memories come to mind that speak deeply to you? Press into those and start your conversation with God.

Lord, what do You want to say to me today?

SOMETHING BETTER—LATER

[Jesus said,] "Anyone who even looks at a woman with lust has already committed adultery with her in his heart."
MATTHEW 5:28 NLT

Have you ever heard of the term *delayed gratification*? This means even when you want to do something now there are reasons to wait. God has many impressive things for us to enjoy, but He designed some things to be time-sensitive. For instance if you're thirteen and want to drive you'll need to wait until you have a learner's permit and an instructor. You might want to go to college, but if you're fifteen, the professors will encourage you to come back in a few years. You'll get there. You just need patience.

Some things are meant to be saved for marriage.

When you accept delayed gratification you give up doing something now in order to have something much better later. Seeing pornography of adult women is something you can't unsee. Those images will stay with you. The reason you should stay away from pornography is God wants you to remain pure for your future wife. She deserves your purity.

Dear God, keep my eyes, heart, and sexuality pure. Because You want me to wait—help me be patient. Thanks for promising something wonderful at the end of the waiting. Amen.

THE UNCOMMON COMMON PRACTICE

*Make this your common practice: Confess your sins to each other
and pray for each other so that you can live together whole
and healed. The prayer of a person living right with God
is something powerful to be reckoned with.*
JAMES 5:16 MSG

In the first hundred years following the death, burial, and
resurrection of Jesus it was the common practice for Christ
followers to discuss their struggles and pray together. Does that
sound strange? Some people call this authentic, truthful, and
realistic Christianity.

Think about the alternative. You keep your struggles hidden,
people find it easy to gossip when they don't know what's really
going on, and praying together seems unnatural.

Maybe that sounds more common today than the first-century
model found in James. God wants us to be honest with each
other, to find someone to share our struggles with, and to pray
with someone we trust. Right living with God means authentically
living your life with those who have the power to encourage your
journey.

*Dear God, it doesn't seem natural to share struggles,
mistakes, and even moments of sin with someone else.
But if that's what You want then help change my thinking so
I can experience the benefits of being authentic with someone
I can learn to trust. I want to be whole and healed. Amen.*

*Religion that God accepts as pure and without fault is this:
caring for orphans and widows who need help,
and keeping yourself free from the world's evil influence.*
JAMES 1:27 NCV

In 2004 seven Ugandan men met under a tree and prayed for God to send someone to bring hope and restoration to their war-torn country. God answered by calling Dr. Tim and Janice McCall to move to Uganda in 2005. They bought land around the tree where the men had been praying, and in 2007 Restoration Gateway was built.

Two and half million orphans fight to survive in Uganda, and Uganda has the highest rate in the world of kids being orphaned from parents who die of AIDS. One in seven children die by the age of five. Restoration Gateway runs an orphanage and employs widows to serve as house parents. Kids are clothed, fed, given a clean and safe place to play, and receive an education and medical care. They also employ men and women to work on the grounds, teaching them a trade and job skills, and they aid the local church with a number of ministries.

To learn more about Restoration Gateway (and how to sponsor a child or donate clothes and supplies!), visit www.restorationgateway.org.

God, thank You for hearing prayers and sending Tim and Janice to Uganda. Please continue to provide for Restoration Gateway so they can reach more and more Ugandans. Grow Your church in Uganda so more people can know You. Amen.

LIMITING THE GRACE MEDS

What shall we say then? Are we to continue in sin
that grace may abound? By no means!
How can we who died to sin still live in it?
ROMANS 6:1–2 ESV

Selfishness says, "I want things my way." God's grace offers forgiveness for selfishness. In fact God's grace will cover any and every sin you commit. That's an amazing gift. So, how should you respond to grace?

Some people look at grace as a way to stop feeling any sorrow or guilt for wrong actions. If God's grace takes care of the payment of sin then maybe there's no need to keep sin under control.

Maybe there's a better way to look at this.

Grace is a bit like great medicine you can use to heal wounds, but it makes no sense to wound yourself intentionally just so you can use the medicine. God's grace *is* able to cover your sin wounds, but avoiding sin means you're grateful for grace, willing to learn from your mistakes, and interested in less spiritual pain.

Dear God, when the Bible tells me to die to self
You're encouraging me to place my ambitions a little lower
on my priority list. That's hard to do when I stand
in the way of Your agenda and demand more grace
medicine. Help me trust Your commands. Amen.

OPEN AND CLOSED DOORS

Show me your paths and teach me to follow; guide me by your truth and instruct me. You keep me safe, and I always trust you.
PSALM 25:4–5 CEV

You have heard the expression: *"When one door closes, another one opens."* Think about doors. They don't open on their own. Most of the doors that you encounter on a daily basis are not automatic. They require someone to open them! If you are a Christian, God is always at work opening doors for you. At times, when He knows that what is on the other side is not best for you, He will close a door. As you pray for God's will in your life, you will become more aware of the opening and closing of doors. You may want to attend a certain school, become a member of a particular group, or be elected to a leadership role. Trust the Lord to open the right doors for you. You only see one piece of the puzzle at a time, but God sees your whole life as a completed jigsaw puzzle before Him. He already knows how the pieces will fit together. When you face the disappointment of a closed door in life, remember that God will open another one. The doors your heavenly Father opens before you are always the right ones.

God, sometimes I am so sad when an opportunity passes me by or when someone else seems to get the things I desire for my own life. Remind me that You are at work behind the scenes. Help me to trust You more. Amen.

A TESTIMONY OF EXCELLENCE

Now Daniel so distinguished himself among the administrators and the satraps by his exceptional qualities that the king planned to set him over the whole kingdom.
DANIEL 6:3 NIV

Daniel is an Old Testament character taken from his home when he was a teenager. He was immediately put to the test. He had to learn to thrive in a new culture with new leaders and different customs. Daniel impressed the leaders and they gave him a key role in their government. Another government arrived and got rid of almost everyone but Daniel. He became a leader in this new government as well. His excellence was noticed by the new leaders.

There's more to his life, but it all comes down to Daniel's allegiance to God, focus on integrity, and commitment to excellence.

Christians should be remembered for the excellence they bring to any project. Even if you work for someone who doesn't follow Jesus you can make an impact by making sure what you do is viewed as excellent work, your attitude is viewed as exceptional, and you show honor to your boss.

Dear God, if our world were a test You would always pass with 100 percent. You're the perfect example of excellence and so Daniel followed You. Help me never settle for good enough. Help me reach for excellence in all You ask me to do. Amen.

UH, GOD?

Be merciful to those who doubt.
JUDE 1:22 NIV

Do you ever have doubts about God? Questions you're afraid to ask? Maybe you feel like voicing your doubts makes you a bad Christian, that your faith isn't very sure if you doubt God. You should just believe, and these niggling doubts and questions are bad, so you stuff them down and hide them.

It's *okay* to have doubts, questions, and concerns about God. Know why? Because doubts make you take a closer look at God. And taking a closer look often leads to growth in your spiritual life and a stronger faith. Jesus doesn't want you to have a blind faith, where you just accept everything about Him because you're told that it's right. Jesus wants you to have a *trusting* faith, where you know Him and His character enough to trust Him without hesitation.

What niggling questions bother you about God? How do you have problems trusting Him because you doubt Him? Dive in to the Bible, ask your youth leaders at church, talk with your parents, and read Christian books until you find satisfying answers. Don't shove your questions aside—wrestle with them until you understand God in a new and deeper way!

*God, help me find answers to my questions and resolve my
doubts about You. Use my wondering thoughts
to help me know You better. Amen.*

UNPLUG

Keep the Sabbath holy. You have six days to do your work,
but the Sabbath is mine, and it must remain a day of rest.
EXODUS 31:14 CEV

※※※※※※※※※※※※※※※※※※※※※※※※※※※※※※※※※※

God created the Sabbath as a time to unplug. No working, no cooking, no chores of any kind. Just a time to gather collectively for worship and to rest and relax.

How well do you unplug each week? Traditionally, we reserve Sundays as a Sabbath, but your Sabbath can be on Saturday or any other day of the week (if you don't have school!). Do you fill up your weekends with sporting events, homework, friends, and activities? Even if you're home and not running around, do you spend your "resting" time glued to the TV, computer, or phone? Instead of interacting with your family or spending time with God, do you stay occupied with Facebook, texting, and other types of social media?

Challenge yourself to unplug this week. Instead of staring at a screen, spend time with your parents and siblings. Have a game night. Read a book for fun. Take a nap. Go for a walk. Take time to slow down and break your normal routine and habits.

Lord, it's so easy to stay busy. Even in my downtime,
it's easy to spend hours watching TV, or scrolling through
my phone. Help me to unplug from my daily life and spend
meaningful time with my family and with You. Amen.

TAKE THE RISK

*"What must I do to inherit eternal life?" . . . [Jesus] said to him,
". . . Sell everything you have and give to the poor, and you will
have treasure in heaven. Then come, follow me." When he heard
this, he became very sad, because he was very wealthy.*
LUKE 18:18, 22–23 NIV

When we seek to follow God, when we pray and listen for His
voice, do we really want to hear what He has to say? It's easy to
pray when all we do is talk to God and ask Him for things. But
it's a little more uncomfortable, maybe even scary, to quiet our
hearts and be still, listening for God's voice and accepting what
He has to say.

What are you afraid to hear from God? What stands in your
way of fully following Him? How has your spiritual growth halted
because you're afraid to hear what He might be asking of you?
God isn't a harsh person who will always demand hard things of
you, but following God does come with a price: you have to be
willing to surrender everything.

Are there things you love more than God—things you're not
willing to give up? Will you take the risk to hear from God and
follow Him?

*God, is there something in my life that's become more important
than You? Is there something I need to surrender
so that I can follow You? Amen.*

ABOUT THE AUTHORS

April Frazier has published more than fifty articles in national magazines and book anthologies such as *Guideposts for Teens*, *Brio & Beyond*, and *God's Way for Teens*. Her readings can be found on pages: 33, 37, 42, 44, 55, 61, 74, 75, 80, 86, 94, 95, 97, 98, 104, 108, 109, 114, 117, 118, 120, 121, 124, 125, 126, 128, 129, 131, 132, 133, 135, 138, 140, 141, 143, 144, 145, 147, 148, 150, 151, 152, 154, 155, 156, 157, 159, 160, 161, 163, 165, 167, 168, 170, 171, 173, 174, 175, 177, 178, 179, 182, 184, 186, 187, 188

Glenn A. Hascall is an accomplished writer with credits in more than one hundred books, including titles from Thomas Nelson, Bethany House, and Regal. His writing has appeared in numerous publications around the globe. He's also an award-winning broadcaster, lending his voice to animation and audio drama projects.His readings can be found on pages: 9, 10, 11, 12, 13, 14, 15, 16, 17, 18, 19, 20, 21, 22, 23, 24, 25, 26, 27, 28, 29, 30, 31, 32, 34, 35, 36, 38, 39, 40, 41, 43, 45, 46, 47, 48, 49, 50, 51, 52, 53, 54, 56, 57, 58, 59, 60, 62, 63, 64, 65, 66, 67, 68, 69, 70, 71, 72, 73, 76, 77, 78, 79, 81, 82, 83, 84, 85, 87, 88, 89, 90, 91, 92, 93, 96, 99, 100, 101, 102, 103, 105, 106, 107, 110, 111, 112, 113, 115, 116, 119, 122, 123, 127, 130, 134, 136, 137, 139, 142, 146, 149, 153, 158, 162, 164, 166, 169, 172, 176, 180, 181, 183, 185

SCRIPTURE INDEX